Happy Birthday Dear Alice

&

Stella by Starlight

D0813380

HAPPY BIRTHDAY DEAR ALICE

& STELLA BY STARLIGHT

BERNARD FARRELL

MERCIER PRESS

MERCIER PRESS
PO Box 5, 5 French Church Street, Cork
and
16 Hume Street, Dublin

Trade enquiries to CMD DISTRIBUTION,
55a Spruce Avenue, Stillorgan Industrial Park, Blackrock, Dublin

© Bernard Farrell, 1997

ISBN 1 85635 180 7

10 9 8 7 6 5 4 3 2 1

A CIP record for this book is available from the British Library.

Happy Birthday Dear Alice and *Stella by Starlight*
are copyright plays and may not be performed without a
licence. All rights whatsoever in these plays are strictly
reserved and application for performance, etc., should be
made before rehearsals start to Rosica Colin Limited, 1
Clareville Grove Mews, London SW7 5AH. No performance
may be given unless a licence has been obtained.

The Arts Council
An Chomhairle Ealaíon

Printed in Ireland by Colour Books Ltd.

CONTENTS

PREFACE   7

HAPPY BIRTHDAY DEAR ALICE   9

STELLA BY STARLIGHT   97

PREFACE

In the early 1990s, I was learning all about nursing homes. And so were most of my friends. This was not because we were all in need of care – but because our aged parents had now moved up to the top of the queue. Ahead, for them, lay possible years of fear – and, for us, probable years of guilt.

Our family had just one remaining parent – our mother. Our father had slipped quietly away in the late 1970s. Our mother, however, clearly decided to stay around awhile – and, in those lilac days, we merrily promised her that, no matter what, she'd never enter a nursing home. But, closer to the end, there were darker days when we thought we might be forced to reconsider. However, the chalice was passed from us. She went from hospital to the Carmelite Sisters where, days later, she peacefully decided to follow my father. As she might have put it: 'Better late than never'.

And so, in 1993, when Jim Nolan of Red Kettle Theatre Company commissioned a new play, I knew exactly what I needed to write about. However, it surprised me that I didn't want to write from the perspective of the children being forced to decide, but from the elderly parent being forced to go.

I knew, early on, that it would be a comedy. With me, the darker the subject the more comical it threatens to become. But I also wanted to juggle with time – to show the old lady in her joyous past as well as in her stressful present. And I particularly wanted her dilemma to be counter-pointed by celebration. Hence, her birthday parties.

The play opened in the elegant Theatre Royal in Waterford, directed by Paul Brennan with all his creative energy firmly in place. And, some months later we all shared, with *Alice*, her national tour, her transfer to Dublin and her hundredth continuous performance.

Throughout the writing of *Alice* – and, indeed, the writing of my previous two plays – I had harboured an unfulfilled promise to

Michael Colgan of the Gate Theatre and he had an unfulfilled promise to me. Put simply: I promised to write a play for him and he promised to stage it. And, in 1995, we both set out to keep our promises.

Again, I wanted to write about a woman struggling against the odds – but, unlike Alice, she would be a young woman with her whole life ahead of her, with everything to lose. Her name would be Stella, married to a man who, forced into early retirement, would whisk her of to live in the wilds of Wicklow, where he could pursue *his* hobbies, leaving her to slowly vegetate with, as she would say, 'only the sheep and the goats to complain to'.

Michael loved this idea – entrapment and escape – and, for the first time in my writing career, I shared with someone (him), the day-to-day agonies of play-writing. We kept in close (and often hilarious) contact throughout the writing and re-writing – I testing his confidence, he testing my judgement.

I finished the play in early 1996 – and, within weeks, Michael was telling me that the script was attracting a wonderful cast and that Ben Barnes – by now almost a veteran interpreter of my plays – had agreed to direct. Then, fulfilling his promise, Michael announced that we would be the Gate's presentation in the 1996 Dublin Theatre Festival. That, I felt, showed a lot of trust in me and in *Stella* – and so, within the festival run of the play, I was delighted when it received the award as Best Irish Production. It seemed that I owed that to the Gate, in return.

So, two plays about two very different women. And with this publication, may future productions allow them to go out into the world to re-live their entrapment and devise their escape, each in their own determined way.

BERNARD FARRELL

8

HAPPY BIRTHDAY DEAR ALICE

This play was first produced by Red Kettle Theatre Company at The Theatre Royal Waterford on 26 July 1994 with the following cast:

ALICE	Anna Manahan
JIMMY	Brendan Cauldwell
BARBARA	Noelle Brown
BARRY	Brian Doherty
CORMAC	Arthur Riordan
SANDY	Natalie Stringer
DIRECTOR	Paul Brennan
DESIGNER	Ben Hennessy
LIGHTING	Jim Daly

FOR ALL THE 'ALICES' AND ALL THE 'JIMMYS' OF THIS WORLD

ACT ONE

THE KITCHEN OF ALICE'S HOUSE. A WINDOW AT THE BACK. DOOR TO THE BACK GARDEN AT UP-STAGE-LEFT. DOOR FROM HALLWAY (CALLED THE KITCHEN DOOR) AT STAGE-RIGHT.

THE KITCHEN IS OLD-FASHIONED. A SINK, GAS-STOVE, CUPBOARD, A TALL UTILITY PRESS, A TABLE AND SOME KITCHEN CHAIRS. THERE IS ALSO AN EASY CHAIR AND A GRAMOPHONE – SUGGESTING THAT THE KITCHEN IS ALSO USED AS A LIVING-ROOM. A PICTURE – 'BUBBLES' BY MILLAIS – PROMINENT ON THE WALL. A TELEPHONE, NOW COVERED BY AN ORNATE TEA-COSY, BESIDE THE EASY CHAIR.

IT IS A SUMMER'S AFTERNOON. THE BACK DOOR IS OPEN. SUN STEAMS IN. BIRDSONG. ALICE, HERE AGED 38, IS CAREFULLY TAKING A RECORD FROM ITS COVER. THE YEAR IS 1961.

ALICE: *(SINGS QUIETLY AND HAPPILY)* 'I'm forever blowing bubbles, Pretty bubbles in the air, They reach so high, They nearly touch the sky, Then like my dreams they fade and die ...'
          (JIMMY COMES TO THE BACK DOOR. HE IS ALSO NOW 38. HE WEARS OLD OVERALLS. HE HAS AN OBVIOUS HEARING-AID. HE CARRIES A BAG OF PLASTERER'S TOOLS. HE IS A QUIET, RESERVED MAN)

JIMMY: *(TENTATIVELY)* Excuse me.

ALICE: *(STOPS SINGING)* Oh sorry, I didn't see you.

JIMMY: I was looking for Walter.

ALICE: You're the new man, are you?

JIMMY: That's right – Jimmy Heffernan.

ALICE: Well Jimmy, Walter will be down in a minute – he's still shaving, I think. Did you close the back gate?

JIMMY: No, I don't have one.

ALICE: Pardon me?

JIMMY: I don't have a black cat – did you find a black cat?

ALICE: No, did you lose a black cat?

JIMMY: No, that's what I just said: I don't have one. *(THEN)* Excuse me, did you ask me originally did I lose a

11

	black cat?
ALICE:	No, I said did you close the back gate.
JIMMY:	Ah blast it – it's this hearing aid ... *(ADJUSTING IT)*
ALICE:	Oh I'm sorry, I wasn't aware ...
JIMMY:	The hearing went on the Normandy beaches.
ALICE:	Pardon?
JIMMY:	The war, D-Day, a shell exploded, the hearing went and I've been picking things up wrong ever since. *(HAVING ADJUSTED IT)* There, that's better.
ALICE:	Oh good. *(THEN)* So you did close the back gate after you, did you?
JIMMY:	Oh yes, I did.
ALICE:	We don't want dogs dirtying the garden – Walter may have told you, we have a small baby.
JIMMY:	Ah that's lovely.
ALICE:	Yes, a little girl of eleven months. *(THEN)* And you?
JIMMY:	Oh Andrew is a lovely name – and no doubt in time that'll be shortened to Andy.
ALICE:	No, not Andrew – she's a girl. We've called her Barbara.
JIMMY:	Oh right.
	(AWKWARD PAUSE)
ALICE:	*(THEN)* And are you married?
JIMMY:	Oh yes. Me and Mona, soon as the war ended we tied the knot.
ALICE:	Lovely – and how many children do you have? *(LOUDER)* Children?
JIMMY:	Oh none – wasn't God's will.
ALICE:	Ah. We never thought we'd have any – I married late because I was here minding mammy here.
JIMMY:	Ah.
ALICE:	Then unfortunately, she died up in the nursing home – the big grey building with the small windows that ...
JIMMY:	Oh I know it well – Mona, my wife, is often up there, looking after the dead. She works for Ryan's the Undertakers – she loves anything to do with funerals.
ALICE:	Oh. *(WITH THE RECORD)* I was going to play this record – it's a song mammy used to sing – 'I'm Forever Blowing Bubbles'.

JIMMY: Oh that goes back to circa 1916 and you may be famil-
iar with the painting that inspired it – 'The Bubble
Boy' by Millais.

ALICE: *(GENTLY)* You seem to know a great deal.

JIMMY: Deed I don't – I'm qualified at nothing.

ALICE: Oh Walter says you're great.

JIMMY: Now he's a qualified plumber.

ALICE: But he said you're great at the tiling.

JIMMY: *(STOPS)* Pardon me?

ALICE: At the tiling – he said you're great at the tiling.

JIMMY: Oh I thought you said I was great at the toilet. Yes,
admittedly, but I'm not qualified, per se.

ALICE: Well, you knew about the painting and the song. I'll
play it now.

JIMMY: When Edison invented the gramophone, his first re-
cording was 'Mary had a little lamb'. It's an interesting fact.

ALICE: You really should go on 'Twenty Questions'.
(THE MUSIC BEGINS)
(AS IT PLAYS) Mammy loved that. When she was in
that nursing home – where she should never have
been – I sung it to her even though the nurses said I
was wasting my time because mammy couldn't hear
me anymore – but with that, didn't she smile up at
me because she recognised the song.

JIMMY: *(LISTENING)* It has a grand melody.

ALICE: And the other day, I sang it to Barbara and she smiled
up at me the very same way.

JIMMY: I must see if I can get you a copy of that Bubble Boy
picture – I think you'd like to have it.
(A DOOR CLOSES LOUDLY)

ALICE: Oh God, that's Walter – he's gone out the front door.

JIMMY: What?

ALICE: Quick, go after him ... *(INDICATES THE KITCHEN
DOOR)*

JIMMY: No I'll go around the back ... *(INDICATES THE BACK
DOOR)*

ALICE: No, come through the house ...

JIMMY: No, I wouldn't ... *(GOING)*

ALICE: Quick – Walter will think you're gone.

JIMMY: *(STOPS)* What's that?

ALICE: Hurry – he'll think you're gone.

JIMMY: *(ANXIOUSLY)* I thought you said 'Walter will sing the song!'

            (JIMMY GOES QUICKLY. ALICE SMILES AT HIS CONFUSION. SHE SITS INTO THE EASY CHAIR, LISTENING TO THE MUSIC. THEN THE KITCHEN DOOR OPENS AND BARBARA LOOKS IN. SHE IS 32, WELL-DRESSED, HIGHLY-STRUNG AND HYPER-ACTIVE. SHE SMOKES AND NOW HOLDS A BOTTLE AND A GLASS OF WINE)

BARBARA: Mammy, are you all right?

            (IMMEDIATELY, A CRACK OF THUNDER AND EVERYTHING SUDDENLY CHANGES: THE BACK DOOR SLAMS SHUT. SECURITY BARS LOCK INTO PLACE ON THE WINDOW. THE SUNSHINE IS REPLACED BY RAIN. THE KITCHEN IS VERY GLOOMY. THE MUSIC HAS STOPPED.

            THE FOREGOING WAS ALICE'S MEMORY. NOW SHE HAS PUT ON HER GLASSES AND HER DEMEANOUR/MOVEMENT NOW SHOWS HER PRESENT-DAY AGE: 70, BUT WELL ABLE TO GET AROUND)

BARBARA: Mammy, what are you doing in here in the dark? *(TURNS ON THE LIGHTS)* There, that's better. *(GOES TO ALICE)* Was it all getting a bit much for you in there?

ALICE: A bit tired.

BARBARA: Of course you are – there wasn't a word out of you, was there? – and I know, you were thinking about daddy again, weren't you? Birthdays do that, don't they?

ALICE: You don't remember him at all, do you, Barbara?

BARBARA: Well, I was only two when he was ... *(CORRECTS)* when he passed on. Now you come back in because we are all waiting for you to (blow out the candles) ...

ALICE: It was a terrible death Barbara.

BARBARA: Of course it was – and there still isn't a day that I'm not reminded of him. Now, you come ...

ALICE: Why, do they have bulls in San Francisco?

14

BARBARA: Bulls? No no, I don't mean being reminded of how he died ...

ALICE: I was watching a farming programme the other night ...

BARBARA: Mammy, you shouldn't be watching farming pro-grammes ...

ALICE: And as soon as I saw them bulls ...

BARBARA: You should be thinking of him alive, mammy ...

ALICE: If only he'd've kept running ...

BARBARA: *(PATIENTLY)* Mammy, please – Cormac and I have come a long way for your birthday and it's very dis-appointing if you just sit in there saying nothing and then, when we light your candles, you disappear in here to think about bulls ...

ALICE: It's cosy in here ...

BARBARA: ... and tomorrow we have to see Cormac's parents in Donegal and then we're back to the States and Barry and what's-her-name will be back to England and, just like last year, no arrangements will have been made for you – and we don't want that again this year, do we? So you come back in and blow out your candles ...

ALICE: You and Cormac should have stayed here and rested yourselves before ...

BARBARA: We are rested and Cormac wanted to visit his other relations in ...

ALICE: And hasn't he done great in America ... *(STANDS)*

BARBARA: Yes he has. *(HELPS ALICE)* That's better ...

ALICE: Although he still grinds his teeth, Barbara ...

BARBARA: He doesn't grind his teeth. *(AS ALICE TURNS TO-WARDS THE BACK DOOR)* Where are you off to now?

ALICE: Out to the toilet.

BARBARA: For God's sake, there are two toilets *inside* this house.

ALICE: This is handier – and tell them to bring the cake in and I'll blow out the candles here.

BARBARA: *(ANGRILY)* Mammy, you did this last year and we never got around to making any arrangements ...
(ALICE HAS TAKEN AN UMBRELLA AND GONE OUT INTO THE BACK GARDEN. WE SEE HER PASS

THE WINDOW)

BARBARA: *(TO HERSELF)* Give me patience this day.
(AS ALICE GOES, BARRY COMES IN. HE IS 30 AND CONFIDENT, DRESSED IN A 3-PIECE SUIT, LOOK-ING PROSPEROUS. SMOKES. HE HOLDS A GLASS OF WHISKEY)

BARRY: *(HIGH-SPIRITED. SINGING)* Happy Birthday to you ... *(THEN)* Where's ma disappeared to now?

BARBARA: Gone to the outside toilet.

BARRY: What?

BARBARA: It's a wonder she doesn't sleep in a cardboard box out there.

BARRY: Jesus, what kind of a life does she live here.

BARBARA: Well you tell me, Barry – you're in England, I'm 6,000 miles away.

BARRY: *(BACKS DOWN)* I know that, Barbara, and I do worry about her – Sandy says I worry too much – she said it just now.

BARBARA: So how often do you see her?

BARRY: *(PROUDLY)* Oh every night if I can – she loves the night-life and the club-scene ...

BARBARA: I mean Mammy for Christ sake – how often do you see mammy?

BARRY: Oh – well not as often as I'd like, over there it takes time to get established – like the selling game is high-ly competitive ...

BARBARA: Last year, I thought we'd all decided she needed looking-after ...

BARRY: Oh absolutely.

BARBARA: ... and we all left without doing anything – but this year a nursing home will have to be picked – unless you want to wait until she falls and needs round-the-clock medical care?

BARRY: No, no, agreed – absolutely – and Sandy agrees too – Sandy says she definitely needs looking-after.

BARBARA: *(COLDLY)* Does she? And what does Valerie say?

BARRY: Valerie?

BARBARA: *(ANGRILY)* Valerie your wife, Valerie the mother of your children ...

BARRY: Okay, okay ...

BARBARA:	Valerie that you promised to love for the rest of your life!
BARRY:	You don't like Sandy much, do you?
BARBARA:	How could I? I don't know her ...
BARRY:	And you're making no effort to know her ...
BARBARA:	... and neither do you know her – but then how could you: when you married Valerie, she was probably still in Pampers. It's bloody ridiculous, Barry.
BARRY:	It's not if you knew what Valerie was doing to me.
BARBARA:	She was too good for you.
BARRY:	Telling me that everything was my fault – saying, last Christmas, in front of our two daughters, that she suspected I was a closet homosexual?
BARBARA:	What?
BARRY:	But Sandy proved her wrong there – Sandy, with no university degrees, Sandy who left school at sixteen ...
BARBARA:	Sandy!
BARRY:	She proved to me that, in that very department, I'm the best ever – as Sandy says: with me it's a First Division performance every time.
BARBARA:	For God's sake! *(GOING)* I'm getting the others in here.
BARRY:	In here?
BARBARA:	Well mammy says she's not moving ... *(GOING)*
BARRY:	Oh right. Then Sandy and I will be going ...
BARBARA:	*(SHARPLY)* Barry, no one's going until we sort out mammy ...
BARRY:	All right, but then we're going.
BARBARA:	Yes, can't wait to get back to the First Division. *(GOES)* *(BARRY LOOKS AROUND. THEN ALICE APPEARS OUTSIDE WITH HER UMBRELLA. SHE COMES IN, CAREFULLY LOCKING THE BACK DOOR)*
BARRY:	Ah ma – are you all right?
ALICE:	Grand, Barry.
BARRY:	It's a great party – Sandy and I didn't eat that much because we'll be going out to eat, Sandy and me.
ALICE:	All right, Barry.
BARRY:	But you liked the birthday present we gave you, didn't you?

ALICE: It was grand – did Valerie pick that?

BARRY: What? No no, that was all Sandy's idea – Sandy said we'll get your mother a coffee-maker that'll wake her up every morning by the radio coming on and a piping hot cup of cappuccino being poured out so she won't fall asleep again. I said I'd never have thought of that.

ALICE: *(UNENTHUSIASTIC)* Aye and neither would I.

BARRY: There you are. *(TENTATIVELY)* What do you think of her, by the way? – Sandy.

ALICE: Oh she'll make a good wife for some young-fella some day.

BARRY: *(DEFLATED)* Yeah. I'll get the others in.

ALICE: If they feel cold, we can turn on the gas.

BARRY: Right. And don't forget it was Sandy who picked the coffee-maker.

ALICE: How could I – won't I be thinking of her every morning when it wakes me up.

BARRY: *(HAPPILY)* Exactly. *(GOES)*
(AS SOON AS BARRY CLOSES THE KITCHEN DOOR, WE HEAR THE MUSIC OF 'I'M FOREVER BLOWING BUBBLES' ON A TINKLING PIANO, IN THE DISTANCE ... AS ALICE BEGINS TO REMEM-BER. A SHAFT OF SUNLIGHT APPEARS IN THE BACK GARDEN AND, IN IT, STANDS, JIMMY. HE LOOKS THE SAME AS BEFORE ... BUT WITH A NEW HEARING AID. HE TAPS ON THE DOOR, OPENS IT [DESPITE ITS PRESENT-DAY LOCKS] AND COMES BRISKLY IN)

ALICE: Ah Jimmy, Walter is outside in the van.

JIMMY: Yes, he says he must have left his sandwiches behind ...

ALICE: No, I put then in his bag, at the bottom ...

JIMMY: Oh right ... *(GOING)*

ALICE: Tell him not eat the cheese if he doesn't want.

JIMMY: *(STOPS)* I like cheese myself – unfortunately, Mona hates it.

ALICE: Jimmy, your hearing-aid, it's gone.

JIMMY: No, I've a new one – look, around the back of the ear.

ALICE: Isn't that great – and is it better at hearing than the

18

	other one?
JIMMY:	Pardon me?
ALICE:	*(CAREFULLY)* Is-it-an-improvement?
JIMMY:	Oh yes, I can hear everything now.
ALICE:	Well isn't that great.
JIMMY:	It is, except at night when I take it off, it can contribute to some embarrassing misunderstandings ...
ALICE:	I suppose so but ...
JIMMY:	An example would be ...
ALICE:	... Walter will be waiting ...
JIMMY:	... Mona waking me at three o'clock the other morning to inform me that she wanted a daughter. Well, what could I do but sit up and explain to her that that's all God's will and we'd been over that ground a hundred times and now could she forget about it and go back to sleep. And with that, up she jumps and out of the bedroom, and I didn't know where the blazes she was going ...
ALICE:	*(ENJOYING IT)* Not to the man next door, I hope.
JIMMY:	*(SERIOUSLY)* Pardon me?
ALICE:	*(BACKS DOWN)* No, I was wondering if you knew where she was going?
JIMMY:	That's what I'm saying, I didn't – then back she came carrying a tumbler in her hand. She hadn't said she wanted a daughter, she said she wanted water.
ALICE:	*(LAUGHS)* Oh dear.
JIMMY:	*(SOLEMNLY)* Yes, Walter was amused too.
ALICE:	Yes and now he'll be waiting for you.
JIMMY:	Right – we're fixing Mrs McCarthy's cistern today.
ALICE:	Then you be careful of the bull.
JIMMY:	The what?
ALICE:	They have a bull in their back field.
JIMMY:	We won't be near it – but there's an interesting thing about bulls: bulls are in fact colour-blind and ...
ALICE:	Walter is waiting, Jimmy.
JIMMY:	Oh right, yes – and he needn't eat the cheese if he doesn't want to.

(JIMMY GOES. ALICE GOES TO THE BACK DOOR, ALLOWING THE SUN ON HER FACE. SHE CONTENTEDLY CLOSES THE BACK DOOR AND

*COMES IN AND SITS IN HER CHAIR. SUDDENLY
THE KITCHEN DOOR OPENS. IMMEDIATELY, THE
SUNLIGHT DISAPPEARS, THE MUSIC STOPS –
AND BARBARA, CORMAC, BARRY AND SANDY
NOISILY ENTER.*

*CORMAC IS 40, IN AMERICAN CLOTHES, WITH
AN ADOPTED AMERICAN ACCENT. HE NOW
CARRIES THE BIRTHDAY CAKE WITH ITS CAND-
LES LIT AND HE HAS AN ELABORATE FLASH-
CAMERA AROUND HIS NECK.*

*SANDY IS 17, ATTRACTIVE, SEXILY DRESSED
AND IS ENGLISH. SHE NOW CARRIES A TRAY OF
CUPS AND TEA. BARBARA CARRIES MANY
GLASSES AND MORE BOTTLES. BARRY IS TRY-
ING TO CARRY HIS DRINK AND TICKLE SANDY
AT THE SAME TIME.*

*ALICE IS AGAIN OLD AND WEARING HER
GLASSES. ALL AROUND HER NOW EXPLODES
INTO HEIGHTENED ACTIVITY)*

CORMAC: Okay, where is she hiding?

BARBARA: Mammy, I got them all in ...

CORMAC: Mohammed comes to the mountain, mother.

BARRY: *(TICKLING SANDY)* Tickle, tickle tickle.

SANDY: Stop it, Barry!

BARBARA: Put the cake down there, Cormac.

CORMAC: *(HOLDING THE CAKE)* Hey, this room has changed.

BARBARA: Put the cake down, Cormac.

BARRY: *(PURSUING SANDY)* And no tickles here?

SANDY: *(GIGGLING, WITH THE TRAY)* Barry! Stop it!

CORMAC: Are all those bars necessary?

BARRY: *(TICKLING)* Pretending she hates it!

BARBARA: *(ANNOYED)* Cormac, will you put that cake down
           before you ...

SANDY: *(SCREAMS)* Stop it, Barry!
           *(SANDY HAS JUMPED ASIDE AND HIT INTO COR-
           MAC. ALL RUSH TO SAVE THE CAKE)*

CORMAC: Look out!

BARBARA: *(SCREAMS)* Jesus Christ, Cormac!

CORMAC: Okay, I've got it ... *(JUGGLES WITH IT)*

BARRY: I have it ... I have it ...

CORMAC: *(ANGRILY TO BARRY)* Leave it, I have it.

BARRY: Got it! *(PUTS THE CAKE ON THE TABLE)*

BARBARA: *(FURIOUS TO CORMAC)* I told you to put it down, why didn't you put it down.

CORMAC: I got bumped into!

BARBARA: If the cake was put down, it wouldn't have mattered.

CORMAC: It's down now, relax honey. Look, I'll re-light the candles.

BARBARA: *(QUIETER)* And stop grinding your teeth.

CORMAC: I'm not! *(LIGHTS THE CANDLES)*

BARRY: *(LIGHTLY TO SANDY)* Think I hit the trigger spot there.

SANDY: *(GIGGLING)* That was all your fault.

BARBARA: *(TO BARRY)* And would you grow up, for Christ sake!

CORMAC: It's okay, honey, relax. Mother, are you sure you want to stay in here?

BARBARA: She does! Let's sing the birthday song now ...

CORMAC: But it's like Alcatraz in here. *(TAKES A PHOTO)*

BARBARA: *(IMPATIENTLY)* Mammy wants it that way.

BARRY: *(TO CORMAC)* Because the houses on each side were burgled and ...

BARBARA: Which we'll be discussing later. Now, before the day is gone, can we have the birthday song. *(BEGINS TO SING)* 'Happy ...'

CORMAC: *(OF THE STOVE)* That's not gas, is it?

BARBARA: Cormac, can we have the song before that damn cake burns the place down.

SANDY: *(SMALL VOICE)* That nearly happened to my sister once.

BARBARA: *(HARD)* What? Did you say something, Candy?

BARRY: Her name is Sandy.

BARBARA: Did you say something?

SANDY: *(AFRAID)* No, nothing, it was nothing.

BARRY: No, say it, darling – what was it?

SANDY: *(EMBARRASSED)* It was nothing.

CORMAC: No, you say it right out.

SANDY: It was different to what you were saying.

BARRY: We'd still like to hear it, sweetheart.

CORMAC: I think she's going to tell us.

BARBARA: And will I phone the Fire Brigade while she's making up her mind?

BARRY: For God's sake, Barbara!

CORMAC: Or why don't we wait until after mother blows out the candles?

BARRY: That's a great idea – okay, ma, up you get and blow out your candles.
(ALICE GETS UP TO COME TO THE TABLE)

BARBARA: For God's sake, the blowing out of the candles comes *after* we sing the Birthday Song. Sit down, mammy!

CORMAC: Save your breath, mother, the song comes first.
(ALICE STOPS AND RETREATS BACK TO HER CHAIR)

BARRY: Back you go, ma. *(TO SANDY)* Then you can say what you said, darling.

SANDY: *(QUIETLY)* It was only about my sister, Darlene ...

CORMAC: *(LOUDLY)* Okay folks, let's raise that roof.

ALL: *(SING)* 'Happy Birthday to you/Happy Birthday to you/Happy Birthday dear Alice/Happy Birthday to you.'
(CHEERS)

BARBARA: And now, mammy ...

BARRY: Up you get, ma.

CORMAC: We want a big blow ...
(ALICE HAS COME TO THE TABLE AND BLOWS OUT THE CANDLES. BARBARA IMMEDIATELY GOES INTO ACTION, CUTTING THE CAKE, PUTTING ON THE KETTLE, ETC., AS)

BARBARA: You can sit back now, mammy.

BARRY: Back you go, ma.

BARBARA: Tea for everyone now.

CORMAC: We still have our drinks, honey.

BARBARA: *(HARD)* Tea for everyone, Cormac.

CORMAC: Fine, honey.
(AS ALICE RETREATS BACK TO HER CHAIR, CORMAC STALKS HER TO TAKE A PHOTO OF HER – ALICE FRIGHTENED BY THE STALKING AND BY THE FLASH INTO HER FACE. THEN)

CORMAC: *(OF THE PHOTO)* Nice shot there – might sell that one.

SANDY: *(TO BARBARA)* Let me do that. *(MAKE THE TEA)*
BARBARA: We can manage, Randy.
SANDY: It's Sandy.
BARBARA: *(NOW CUTTING THE CAKE)* And everyone will have a slice, yes?
BARRY: And two slices for Barry, thank you.
CORMAC: Not good for you, pal.
BARRY: My body can take it. Sandy here is a reflexologist ...
SANDY: I'm training to be one ...
BARRY: Okay, but she gave me the once over and I'm okay. Reflexology does not lie.
CORMAC: That's good to know. I just stay fit and absolutely refuse all cakes and cookies.
BARBARA: *(CAKE ON A PLATE)* Eat that, Cormac.
CORMAC: Sure, honey. *(TAKES IT. TO BARRY)* Except on occasions, of course: I'm not a stickler.
BARRY: *(EATS THE CAKE)* I'm glad to hear it because that's why I don't like Americans – they live in extremes, all or nothing at all.
SANDY: I love Americans.
                  (BARBARA IS NOW HURRIEDLY SERVING TEA AND CAKE AND TAKING A ROLL OF KITCHEN TOWEL FROM THE TALL UTILITY PRESS. SHE REPLACES THIS IN THE PRESS. ALL WHILE)
CORMAC: No, Americans got it right, Barry – take my job, Freelance Photography, *(GIVES BARRY HIS CARD)* and that includes straight press shots to portraits to video and my subject matter can be anything from the humble Mexican family to the Hollywood stars ...
BARRY: Nice card. *(HANDS IT BACK)*
CORMAC: You keep it, I got hundreds – and for that you got to stay fit and free and flexible – so you work out, socialise, make contacts, stay in shape and, hey presto, the commissions comes in and you are ready. And that is the American way.
BARBARA: Cormac, put that cosy on the tea-pot, keep it warm.
CORMAC: Sure honey.
                  (CORMAC PICKS UP THE COSY AS ALICE REACHES OUT TO ALERT HIM. HE LIFTS IT. UNDER IT IS THE TELEPHONE. THE INSTRU-

23

MENT FALLS OFF THE CRADLE)

CORMAC: *(AMUSED)* Hey, look what's under the tea-cosy – her telephone.

BARBARA: *(AMUSED)* Oh mammy, are you keeping it warm?

BARRY: *(AMUSED)* She's waiting for a hot telephone call! *(LAUGHTER)*

BARBARA: It's all right, mammy, we'll put it back.

CORMAC: *(PUTS IT BACK)* Bye bye hot line.

BARBARA: *(TO ALICE)* Oh mammy, you really do need looking after, don't you? Indeed you do. *(QUIETLY, TO ALL)* Getting strange. This is what worries me about her. *(SILENCE. AS THEY EAT)*

SANDY: *(TENTATIVELY)* She was wearing a lacy top and the whole thing went up.

CORMAC: Excuse me, Sandy?

SANDY: *(SMALL VOICE)* My sister, Darlene, I was telling you about.

CORMAC: Oh yeah what you were telling us ...

BARRY: Oh yes ...

SANDY: *(SMALL VOICE)* That's what happened to her when her birthday cake set light to the lacy top she was wearing ...

BARRY: God Sandy, that sounds dreadful – everyone hear this, what Sandy was saying about her sister, Darlene?

CORMAC: It sounds really wild.

BARRY: Tell us all about it, sweetheart.

SANDY: Well, it was ...

BARRY: Go right ahead *(QUIETLY)* and take your time and speak up.

CORMAC: Listen to this, mother – Sandy has a story about her sister.

BARRY: Off you go, Sandy, from the beginning – ma, are you listening? *(TO SANDY)* She is.

SANDY: Well, it was her nineteenth birthday and she leaned too near the cake and her top went up and she pulled it off and threw it on a chair and that nearly caught fire only someone put it out but the cake was alight and Darlene's boyfriend, Jason, who she thinks looks like Tom Cruise though we all think he is more like

Mel Gibson, he threw what he thought was a bottle of water onto it, but it turned out it was a bottle of paraffin and the whole thing was in flames ...

(DURING THIS, WE BEGIN TO HEAR THE TINK-LING PIANO, NOW SADLY PLAYING 'I'M FOR-EVER BLOWING BUBBLES'. THEN THE KITCHEN DOOR SLOWLY OPENS. ALICE GOES TO IT. JIMMY STANDS THERE, LOOKING BROKEN-HEARTED, WITH A LIGHT BEHIND HIM. THIS, IN ALICE'S MEMORY, IS UNSEEN BY SANDY WHO WILL FREEZE IN HER STORY TO THE SILENT ATTENT-IVENESS/DELIGHT OF BARRY AND CORMAC AND THE DISGUST OF BARBARA)

JIMMY: *(SADLY)* Alice.

ALICE: *(SADLY)* Ah Jimmy, you were up there a long time.

JIMMY: We said the Rosary. He looks at peace.

ALICE: He does – I was glad I got him home.

JIMMY: You got his comb?

ALICE: No, got him home – from the hospital.

JIMMY: Oh right – but I'm terrible terrible sorry, Alice.

ALICE: Now now, it wasn't your fault

JIMMY: If only I'd heard him ...

ALICE: But how could you?

JIMMY: Bloody batteries had run down, God damn them and you had earlier warned us about the bull ...

ALICE: Who was to know? Will you have something?

JIMMY: I won't – Mona will be down any minute ...

ALICE: Oh Mona was great at the laying out – how can I ever thank her ...

JIMMY: Oh Mona is a god-send at any bereavement – even down at the Undertakers they say she has a great way with corpses.

ALICE: Oh she has.

JIMMY: I noticed that about her when we first met: she's not good with people, but show her a corpse and she comes into her own.

ALICE: Isn't it a great gift.

JIMMY: And poor you and the babby – what's she now?

ALICE: She's two but we'll manage.

JIMMY: Oh and I got you that picture of the bubble boy – and

	about time, sez you.
ALICE:	You shouldn't have bothered.
JIMMY:	I'll drop it over some evening. But you should rest yourself now.
ALICE:	I will, I will.
JIMMY:	Oh he made out a will, did he?
ALICE:	What? Oh yes, Walter – he left me comfortable.
JIMMY:	Ah grand.
ALICE:	And Jimmy, I think he'd've wanted you to take over his business, if you wanted it.
JIMMY:	Ah, I don't know, Alice – but I wonder if you'd mind me dropping in on you from time to time ...?
ALICE:	I'd be disappointed if you didn't.
JIMMY:	Maybe tomorrow night, after the ... the ...?
ALICE:	Funeral, that'd be lovely.
JIMMY:	It's the saddest time. My condolences again, sincerely ...
ALICE:	I know, Jimmy.
JIMMY:	I'll get Mona – she get's terribly attached to the dead.
ALICE:	I'll see you later, Jimmy, and think about Walter's business and his van too. I think he'd've wanted that.
JIMMY:	We'll see. God bless, Alice.

(JIMMY GOES, CLOSING THE DOOR. ALICE RETURNS TO HER CHAIR. THE MUSIC FADES AS THE 'PRESENT' FILTERS BACK TO HER CONSCIOUSNESS AGAIN: LAUGHTER FROM BARRY, CORMAC AND SANDY ON THE COMPLETION OF HER STORY. BARBARA SITS UNSMILING)

CORMAC:	Great story, Sandy – really good.
BARRY:	Once she gets going there's no stopping her.
CORMAC:	*(JOLLY)* Proud of you, Sandy.
BARRY:	And I mean in more ways than one.
SANDY:	*(NOW ENJOYING IT. TO BARRY)* You're going to get me a bad name.
BARRY:	I mean in reflexology – *(TO CORMAC)* that's how we met, you know.
SANDY:	*(TO CORMAC. MERRILY)* He came to my sister, Darlene – who is fully qualified – and he got me.
CORMAC:	You know, I was always curious about reflexology – it's a kind of massage, Sandy, isn't it?

BARBARA: *(CURTLY)* Yes it is – and now that we've had the cake and the birthday song and heard all about Darlene, I think it's time we talked about mammy. *(LOUDER)* About you, mammy.

ALICE: What about me, Barbara – I'm grand.

BARBARA: *(KINDLY)* Now mammy, you went on with this last year ...

CORMAC: Making that speech about how you'd never put Barbara or Barry into a nursing home ...

BARRY: And I said I'd love to be in a nursing home – if the nurses were sexy enough! *(TICKLES SANDY)*

BARBARA· Can we please keep to the point. *(TO ALICE)* But I think you realise now, mammy, that it is all for your own good – so let us proceed.

BARRY: Then Sandy and I will be slipping away.

BARBARA: But not before, Barry! So to begin, I think, Cormac, that you have some initial points to make.

CORMAC: Me?

BARBARA: And some brochures to show mammy.

CORMAC: Oh I left them in the car.

BARBARA: *(CONTROLLED)* You left them in the car?

CORMAC: I didn't think we'd be doing that now ...

BARBARA: *(ANGRILY)* Give me the keys, I'll get them ...

CORMAC: No honey, I can ...

BARBARA: The keys, Cormac – I'll get the damn things.

CORMAC: I locked them in the glove compart ...

BARBARA: *(TAKES THE KEYS)* I'll find them. *(QUIETLY)* I'm damned if I'm letting another year go by.
(BARBARA GOES ANGRILY THROUGH THE KITCHEN DOOR)

BARRY: *(TO CORMAC)* She's got very highly strung.

CORMAC: Yeah – kids.

BARRY: Pardon?

CORMAC: She'd like a family – kids.

BARRY: Oh – and you wouldn't ...?

CORMAC: No we both would, and can. Just down to timing – but we'll get there.

BARRY: Course.

CORMAC: *(LOUDLY TO ALICE)* Just getting some brochures I think you'll like , mother.

BARRY:	*(LOUDLY)* Get you fixed up.
CORMAC:	*(LOUDLY)* Really good places. *(TO BARRY, OF ALICE)* Very quiet.
BARRY:	*(QUIETLY)* The mind. She loses touch.
CORMAC:	Sure. Seems to like the idea of prison.
	(ALICE NOTICES THESE COMMENTS. NOW SILENCE. THEN)
SANDY:	It's the feet, it's all to do with the feet.
CORMAC:	Sorry, Sandy?
SANDY:	Reflexology – you were asking was it a massage.
BARRY:	Jesus, Sandy – *(TO CORMAC)* – That's my Sandy, never forgets a remark or a question ...
CORMAC:	Hey 'retention of information' – that is very highly regarded in the States ...
SANDY:	Everyone is always amazed that I can continue a conversation that a client started when he was last in, maybe eight weeks before.
BARRY:	Sandy's mind just amazes me.
CORMAC:	You should think of making it to the States, Sandy, you would do very well.
SANDY:	I'd love America ...
CORMAC:	You'd be great out there ...
BARRY:	No no, forget it ...
CORMAC:	No Barry, and you would have come out years ago only Valerie stopped you.
BARRY:	Valerie never stopped me ...
CORMAC:	And I told you that your Valerie is like my Barbara – she needs a firm hand.
BARRY:	Valerie knew I had a firm hand – Jesus, the look on her face the day I walked out.
CORMAC:	Couldn't have been better than the look on Barbara's face the day I *told* her we were going Stateside.
SANDY:	*(JOINING IN)* Or the look on the faces of the girls.
BARRY:	*(STOPS)* What girls?
SANDY:	At Darlene's Health Club the first day you drove me down and they asked me who you were.
BARRY:	*(DELIGHTED)* Oh right – and what did you say?
SANDY:	I said his name is Barry, he's from Ireland, he's married with two daughters and I'm having an affair with him. The looks on their faces, they never thought I'd

	do it – and my mum was disgusted too.
BARRY:	*(ANNOYED)* Disgusted? What's there to be disgusted about?
SANDY:	No, I don't mean disgusted.
BARRY:	You just said disgusted.
SANDY:	I didn't mean disgusted – like the girls certainly weren't disgusted because they kept asking me how did I land you and had you got a twin brother.
BARRY:	*(DELIGHTED)* They asked you that?
SANDY:	But I wouldn't tell them anything except that you were great ... *(INTIMATELY)* ... and great since the first time we ... *(AWARE OF CORMAC)* ... first time we met.
CORMAC:	At the reflexology.
BARRY:	The luckiest day of my life, Cormac.
CORMAC:	It is a kind of massage, isn't it?
BARRY:	It's a helluva massage – you lie down and in comes this one *(SANDY)* big smile, pulls the curtains, puts on the soft music, closes the door and gets down to it.
CORMAC:	*(LECHEROUSLY)* You say no more, buddy, say not one word more – and it's up periscope and we're under way. Wooooo.
BARRY:	No no, don't get me wrong – it's all very respectable.
SANDY:	There's nothing shady about it ...
BARRY:	It's all totally above board ...
CORMAC:	*(BACKS DOWN)* Oh yea, sure – that's what I'm saying ...
BARRY:	Like it's only the feet, all you take off is your shoes and socks ...
CORMAC:	Right – you're only naked from the knee down.
BARRY:	And very professional – you should try it, Cormac – seriously.
CORMAC:	Oh I will – I guess they got them all over San Francisco ...
BARRY:	No, here, now. Slip off your shoe and sock.
CORMAC:	What?
BARRY:	Why not – just give Sandy the feel of your foot – all right with you, Sandy?
SANDY:	I won't be able to tell much with one foot ...
BARRY:	No, just to give him an idea ...

CORMAC: Well thanks very much – but Barbara will be coming back ...
(NOW, QUIETLY, WE HEAR THE TINKLING PIANO PLAYING 'BUBBLES'. IT STAYS UNDER, AS)

BARRY: I'll watch the door – you can easily slip the shoe back on.

CORMAC: *(TAKING OFF HIS SHOE)* But she only went to the car ...

BARRY: I'll hear her – you'll be really amazed at this ...

CORMAC: *(OF ALICE)* But your mother ...

BARRY: She notices nothing – earlier she thought Sandy was Valerie.

CORMAC: Okay – just make sure Barbara doesn't ...

BARRY: She won't. *(GOES TO THE KITCHEN DOOR)*

SANDY: I'll just give it a quick massage ...

CORMAC: *(NERVOUSLY)* Or a quick explanation would be okay.

SANDY: Just relax, let me have your foot and I'll do all the work.
(FROM NOW, IN A FREEZE, BARRY WILL WATCH THE DOOR WHILE SANDY EXAMINES COR-MAC'S FOOT. CORMAC RELAXING NOW.

THE LIGHT IS NOW BRIGHT IN THE BACK GARDEN. OUTSIDE THE BACK DOOR, BARBARA APPEARS. SHE LOOKS YOUNGER. SHE CARRIES A WATERING CAN. ALICE IS MORE SPRITELY)

BARBARA: I thought you were going to the shops.

ALICE: I need time to recover.

BARBARA: Recover from what, for God's sake?

ALICE: From the news that my only daughter, after the great education I gave her, wants to go and marry a beggar-man from Donegal.

BARBARA: Cormac is not a beggar-man – he is a professional photographer.

ALICE: Standing outside the church begging people to let him take their photograph.

BARBARA: Their Confirmation photograph, their wedding photograph ...

ALICE: Mrs Gillespie says he has no film in the camera ...

BARBARA: Then how does he sell them if he has no film?!

ALICE: And I never liked the way he grinds his teeth.

BARBARA: Mammy, that's an awful thing to say.
ALICE: Well it's true – all the dogs bark at him.
BARBARA: The dogs don't bark at him.
ALICE: They do – I always know when he's coming by the barking of every dog in the street and Mrs Gillespie noticed it too.
BARBARA: Mrs Gillespie!
ALICE: And then when he heard that your father was gored by a bull ...
BARBARA: Don't start that again ...
ALICE: It was the first time I ever met him, Barbara, sitting inside, grinding his teeth and every dog barking for miles outside ...
BARBARA: You're making him sound like Dracula ...
ALICE: And when he was told about how your father died ...
BARBARA: He was embarrassed!
ALICE: ... not a word about how did I feel or was I broken-hearted or did your father suffer much pain, but asking me 'And what happened to the bull?'
BARBARA: He didn't say that – he asked was the bull put down because his brother is a vet.
ALICE: *(STOPS)* Who's brother is a vet?
BARBARA: Well hardly the bull's brother – Cormac's!
ALICE: Then why don't you marry him – that's a good job ...
BARBARA: Because he's already married!
ALICE: Of course he is and we all know why the other fellow isn't!
(PAUSE)
BARBARA: *(CONTROLLED)* Will I leave the watering-can in here?
ALICE: *(GENTLY)* Oh Barbara, I only want the best for you.
BARBARA: *(HUGS HER)* I know, mammy. But Cormac is lovely really and he'll be good to me – and we'll have lots of grandchildren for you. You'll see. *(OF THE WATERING-CAN)* So will I leave it here or what?
ALICE: You can put it back outside – I don't feel like watering plants today.
BARBARA: You will later. *(GOING WITH THE CAN)*
ALICE: Get him to stop grinding his teeth before the wedding ...

BARBARA: He doesn't grind his teeth!

ALICE: ... or in the photographs, everyone will think you've married the werewolf.

(BARBARA GOES, RESIGNED, WITH THE CAN. THE MUSIC FADES. THE LIGHT OUTSIDE FADES TO RAIN, ALICE RETURNS TO HER CHAIR AND THE DIALOGUE OF 'THE PRESENT' FADES IN.

SANDY IS MASSAGING CORMAC'S FOOT, HIS TROUSERS ROLLED UP. HE IS ENJOYING IT. BARRY WATCHES THE DOOR)

BARRY: Can you detect any ailments, Sandy?

SANDY: No – I'd say you're very healthy.

CORMAC: Work-out every day – same gym as Robert de Niro.

SANDY: *(WITH HIS FOOT)* You don't jog barefoot, do you?

BARRY: There you are! – she knew immediately I smoked twenty cigs a day.

CORMAC: Jog barefoot all the time – mainly on China Beach.

SANDY: Yes – and your feet are lovely and tanned.

CORMAC: *(ENJOYING THE MASSAGE)* Tanned bodies are pretty common in California – all year round too.

SANDY: I'd love to be tanned all year round.

CORMAC: Barbara hates the sun. I live for it.

SANDY: Me too. And do they have nudist beaches there?

CORMAC: Oh sure – I'm a member of a club. Barbara isn't, but I am.

SANDY: I'd be too.

CORMAC: You really should come out, Sandy. *(CORRECTS)* Both of you.

BARRY: *(COLDLY)* Yeah, okay, thanks. Sandy, you can pack it in now ...

SANDY: *(CONTINUING)* So this tan is all over, is it?

CORMAC: Absolutely all over.

SANDY: That's what I'd love.

CORMAC: You'd fit in quickly Stateside, Sandy.

BARRY: *(COMES FROM THE DOOR. CURTLY)* Okay, Sandy, I said you can leave it at that – I think he's got the idea now.

SANDY: All right, Barry – but just look at his foot.

BARRY: I can see it – it's a foot.

SANDY: But it's so well-formed.

BARRY: And what have I got – horses hooves?

SANDY: Course not, silly ... *(TO CORMAC)* It is a perfect shape – poor Barry has big bunions.

BARRY: *(ANGRILY)* I do not have big bunions.

SANDY: *(MERRILY)* Yes you do – and you had athlete's foot when you first ...

BARRY: Why the hell are you going on about ...?

CORMAC: The Californian sun would cure athlete's ...

BARRY: I don't have athlete's foot!

SANDY: No but you did ...

BARRY: *(FURIOUS)* And will you get your shaggin hands off him and let him put his clothes on.

SANDY: *(ANGRILY)* His clothes *are* on.

BARRY: His shoe and sock then! *(CONTROLLED, TO COR-MAC)* The point is, Cormac, that your Barbara might walk in any minute and ...

CORMAC: Sure, yeah, Barry – good point. That was lovely, Sandy.

SANDY: *(ANNOYED)* Yes, until some people started getting jealous again.

BARRY: *(ANNOYED)* Who's getting jealous ... I wasn't get-ting ...
(A SOUND OUTSIDE)
And here she is, what did I say? *(TO SANDY)* That's the reason – no other.
(CORMAC SETTLES HIMSELF QUICKLY AS BAR-BARA COMES IN, CARRYING BROCHURES AND A PAD)

BARBARA: That woman, Mrs Gillespie – *(LOUDLY)* I was talk-ing to Mrs Gillespie, mammy – questions, questions, questions, you'd think I was in the witness box. Cor-mac, why is your trousers rolled up?

CORMAC: What? Oh, I was scratching my leg.

BARBARA: Well don't. She was asking about you too – where you worked, what time you got up in the morning, did you have a dog ...

CORMAC: A dog?

BARBARA: I think she's gone senile. *(LOUDLY)* Mammy, Mrs Gillespie – has she been well?

BARRY: Barbara, can we get on with it – Sandy and I have a table booked ...

SANDY:	*(ANNOYED)* I'm not going.
BARRY:	*(FURIOUSLY)* The shaggin table is booked for dinner for Christ sake!
SANDY:	I don't want any dinner.
BARRY:	Then don't eat it.
SANDY:	I won't.
BARRY:	Don't! *(QUIETER)* And I don't have bunions.
SANDY:	All right, big deal – you don't have bunions!
BARBARA:	For God's sake, is this all you two have to talk about – dinner and bunions? God be with Valerie. *(HARD)* Now Cormac, I think you have something to say.
CORMAC:	What? Oh sure, Barbara. Well, I feel that Sandy in referring to Barry's bunions was merely ...
BARBARA:	About the brochures and the places you saw! *(SHOVES THE BROCHURES AT HIM)*
CORMAC:	Oh right. Mother – Alice – let me open by saying that this is something that was pursued at your Birthday Party last year but not finalised, and if it had been finalised, we wouldn't be here today but instead you'd be in some bright, clean restful nursing home where you'd be looked-after morning, noon and night ...
BARBARA:	... with no fear of burglars or anything, mammy ...
CORMAC:	... and where you'd meet lots of new friends ...
BARRY:	... and there'd be no need to sell this house ...
BARBARA:	*(SHARPLY)* We'll come to that, Barry.
BARRY:	What?
BARBARA:	*(TO ALICE)* What Cormac's saying is that we are sure that once you see these brochures, you'll be delighted to go. *(ALICE TAKES A BROCHURE)*
SANDY:	Barry, is there a loo?
BARRY:	Top of the stairs and turn right.
BARBARA:	Left.
BARRY:	Oh that's right – left.
SANDY:	Right and left?
BARRY:	No, just left.
SANDY:	Right. *(GOES)*
CORMAC:	And may we say, Alice, that we have always admired your courage in taking difficult decisions in the past ...

BARBARA: But like the rest of us, mammy, you were younger then but now, for your sake and for our peace of mind, the time has come for you to be looked-after.

BARRY: And don't worry, ma, the house won't be sold over your head or anything ...

BARBARA: *(TO BARRY)* We'll come to that!

BARRY: No, I think it's important that she knows it can be kept in the family ...

BARBARA: *(HARD)* How kept in the family?

BARRY: Not sold to pay for the nursing home – maybe rented out ..

BARBARA: Rented out to who?

BARRY: To anyone who ...

BARBARA: Like you?

BARRY: Not necessarily me ...

BARBARA: Excuse me a minute, mammy. Cormac!

(BARBARA, CORMAC AND BARRY MOVE ASIDE. ALICE IDLY LOOKS AT THE BROCHURES)

BARBARA: *(TO BARRY)* You must think that Cormac and I are not only stupid but deaf and blind.

BARRY: What are you talking about?

BARBARA: Valerie has your house – you're in a flat in Basingstoke and wouldn't coming in here suit you very nicely ...

BARRY: And so what – it would mean the house stays in the family.

BARBARA: Over my dead body, Barry and over Cormac's dead body ...

BARRY: What are you going on about?

BARBARA: Her! *(OF SANDY)* I'm talking about her living under this roof.

BARRY: But you're out in California ...

BARBARA: In two years, we will be back in Ireland ...

CORMAC: ... to start a family ...

BARBARA: ... whether to start a family or not! – and this is our family home ...

BARRY: It's my family home too ...

BARBARA: Your family home is with your wife Valerie and not shacked-up with that empty-headed bimbo ...

BARRY: She is not empty-headed ...

CORMAC: No Barbara she's not.

BARBARA: *(ROUNDS ON CORMAC)* Cormac, if you ever contradict me again in front of ...
(SANDY COMES IN)

CORMAC: Ah Sandy.

BARBARA: Sandy.

BARRY: Did you find it all right?

SANDY: Well I first turned right instead of left but then I ...

BARBARA: Great. Now, can we get mammy to first pick a nursing home or another year will have gone by ...

BARRY: But I'm still insisting ...

BARBARA: ... and we'll talk about everything else after that.

CORMAC: Exactly.
(AS THEY TURN TO WHERE ALICE SITS)

CORMAC: *(TO SANDY)* Nice house, isn't it?

SANDY: *(TO CORMAC)* Yes, it's lovely and big and ...

BARBARA: Do you have that brochure, Cormac?

CORMAC: Sorry – oh yes – this is the one we thought best. Spare one for you, Barry.

BARBARA: Now, mammy, Cormac is going to tell us now about this lovely place ...

BARRY: *(LOOKING AT THE BROCHURE)* Chestnut Grove.

CORMAC: And it's only fifteen miles as the crow flies with lovely gardens ...

BARBARA: Just read it out, Cormac ...

CORMAC: Right. I'll read it out for you, mother ...

SANDY: I love the American accent.

CORMAC: Oh thank you, Sandy.

BARRY: Half Ireland talks in an American accent.

SANDY: Yes, but Cormac's is real – it goes ever so deep and dark and ...

BARBARA: Are you going to start, Cormac, or will I do it?
(WHEN CORMAC NOW READS, HIS AMERICAN ACCENT SEEMS MORE PRONOUNCED. SANDY LIKES IT. BARRY DOESN'T. BARBARA INDICATES TO ALICE THE PASSAGE BEING READ. ALICE LOOKS BUT IS UNINTERESTED)

CORMAC: No, Barbara – thank you for that, Sandy. So here goes: 'Welcome to Chestnut Grove – a home from home for those of us who yearn for peace and tranquillity in our later years; a haven for recollection and recovery for those of us who have been beset by a debilitating illness – at all times a sanctuary of rest from the noise and the bustle of life. Here, in Chestnut Grove, corporal and spiritual care is administered by the Sisters of Bethany, medical assistance is provided by our inhouse nurses and visiting doctors and, most important, here new friends can be found and lost friendships established ...

(DURING THIS, THE TINKLING PIANO PLAYING 'BUBBLES' IS HEARD. SUNLIGHT EMERGES OUTSIDE AND JIMMY APPEARS AND KNOCKS. ALICE RISES FROM HER CHAIR AND ADMITS HIM. HE CARRIES A WRAPPED BIRTHDAY PRESENT.

BOTH JIMMY AND ALICE ARE ELDERLY IN THIS MEMORY OF LAST YEAR. AS THE MEMORY ESTABLISHES ITSELF FOR ALICE, CORMAC'S VOICE FADES. ALL THEN IN A FREEZE – AS THOUGH ALICE WERE STILL SITTING IN THE CHAIR)

JIMMY: Is the birthday party over?

ALICE: All gone for another year, Jimmy – Barry and Valerie and my grandchildren were the last to leave.

JIMMY: Did anyone do the washing up for you?

ALICE: Valerie did – Barbara telling me I should have a dishwasher.

JIMMY: That's the Americans ...

ALICE: And then, in the same breath, they had all the brochures out and they were on about the nursing homes again.

JIMMY: Ah, they don't mean it, Alice.

ALICE: Oh they do – but they won't get me into one – I have a plan if they try to force me.

JIMMY: A plan to climb over the wall, is it?

ALICE: No, it's a good plan – when I think of Mammy in that nursing home ...

JIMMY: Ah Alice, you're taking it too serious altogether. Here, to get your mind off it, look: *(GIVES HER THE BIRTHDAY PRESENT)* Happy Birthday from me ... and Mona.

ALICE: Ah Jimmy. What is it? *(OPENS IT)* It's a tea-cosy, is it?

37

(THE TEA-COSY IS IDENTICAL TO THE ONE ON THE TELEPHONE)

JIMMY: It's a telephone cosy – you know how you said the telephone gives you a fright when it rings ...

ALICE: Oh it'd lift you.

JIMMY: That goes over it. Mona got it from a dead woman.

ALICE: Pardon me, Jimmy?

JIMMY: *(CORRECTS)* When the dead woman was alive, of course ... before Mona laid her out – she gave her that.

ALICE: *(LAUGHS)* I'm glad it wasn't *after* she laid her out.

JIMMY: Pardon, What? *(REALISES)* Oh I see, yes, exactly.
(JIMMY AND ALICE LAUGH TOGETHER. AS THEY DO, BARBARA'S VOICE COMES INTO ALICE'S CONSCIOUSNESS. CORMAC AND THE OTHERS WILL NOW ADDRESS THE EMPTY CHAIR, WHILE ALICE STAYS IN A FREEZE WITH JIMMY)

BARBARA: *(DELIGHTED)* Now mammy, that's better – that's a smile – we haven't seen you smile all day.

BARRY: Which bit did you like, ma?

CORMAC: The bit about the rabbits I think.

BARBARA: Oh yes – and there are rabbits there, mammy – we saw them.

CORMAC: In California, we have squirrels.

SANDY: I love squirrels.

BARBARA: *(TO CORMAC)* Don't be confusing her by dragging in squirrels. *(LOUDLY TO ALICE)* Keep that one in mind now mammy – the one with the rabbits – and Cormac will read about another one. Go on, Cormac.

CORMAC: *(PICKS UP ANOTHER BROCHURE)* Okay – oh, this is a real sweetie. Listen to this now. This is called Daffodil Downs Nursing Home. *(READS)* 'Welcome to Daffodil Downs, an eighteenth century restored house in its own grounds ...'
(ALREADY CORMAC'S VOICE IS FADING FROM ALICE'S CONSCIOUSNESS AND HER MEMORY WITH JIMMY CONTINUES)

JIMMY: Well, the point is they're gone now and you're safe for another year.

ALICE: Unless I get a stroke ...

JIMMY: Ah not at all ...

ALICE:	Or I fall or robbers break in and ...
JIMMY:	I'll tell you what I'll do ...
ALICE:	They broke in next door ...
JIMMY:	I'll put bars up on that window and locks on the door so they'll never get in.
ALICE:	And supposing there's a fire and I can't get out?
JIMMY:	Now there's an interesting thing about fires: the witches they burned to death in the Spanish Inquisition, never died of burning, but of suffocation, caused by the fire.
ALICE:	*(RELAXED)* Ah well that puts my mind at ease. Instead of being burned to death, I'll only be suffocated
JIMMY:	Ah no, what I'm saying is ...
ALICE:	I know, Jimmy – the bars would be grand and I'm also thinking of bringing my comfortable chair in here ...
JIMMY:	Exactly – and you have the gas to keep you warm ...
ALICE:	And the toilet outside and I'll close off the other rooms and I'll be grand.
JIMMY:	Now you're talking – and Mona and me would never let them take you anywhere, no matter what your plan is.
ALICE:	I know you wouldn't, Jimmy.
JIMMY:	Now, let me get that chair in for you.
ALICE:	Ah no, it's very heavy ...
JIMMY:	I'll manage it – you wait here.
ALICE:	*(LIGHTLY)* Don't strain your back – and have Mona wondering what I have you doing here.
JIMMY:	*(STOPS)* Pardon me, Alice – I'm getting a bit of interference here. *(HIS HEARING-AID)*
ALICE:	*(RECOVERS)* I was just saying that maybe you'd put your present with all my other presents, in the front-room.
JIMMY:	*(TAKES THE COSY AND THE WRAPPINGS)* You will use it, won't you?
ALICE:	Of course I will – isn't it a God-send.
	(JIMMY GOES OUT TO THE HALL, CLOSING THE KITCHEN DOOR BEHIND HIM. THE LIGHT RETURNS TO RAIN. THE MUSIC FADES. ALICE SITS

INTO HER CHAIR.

NOW THE VOICES OF BARBARA, CORMAC, BARRY AND SANDY HAVE BEEN AGAIN CREEPING INTO HER CONSCIOUSNESS)

CORMAC: ... and while Daffodil Downs seems excellent, my own personal recommendation would be Chestnut Grove ...

BARBARA: I think you liked that one best, mammy ...

CORMAC: And don't worry about the cost ...

BARRY: *(TO CORMAC)* She has most of the cover ...

BARBARA: We know she has. So which one would you prefer, mammy – there are vacancies in both and all you have to do is select one and I'll make the phone-call and someone will be over in two hours to help you with all the arrangements. Now, could anything be easier?

(SILENCE. ALICE LOOKS IDLY AT THE BROCHURE)

SANDY: Perhaps she wants to stay here?

BARBARA: *(FURIOUS)* Would you mind shutting up?

SANDY: My granny lives at home ...

BARBARA: I said shut-up ...

BARRY: Now you wait a minute, Barbara ...

BARBARA: *(QUIET AND FURIOUS TO BARRY)* I will not wait a minute – or maybe you want to be the one who gets the phone call to say she's fallen and will be half-paralysed for the next ten years. Who's gong to mind her then? – you? Me? Her? *(SANDY)* Or maybe she'll send her bloody granny over to help her! Use what brains you have, for Christ sake!

BARRY: *(TO SANDY)* Now that's what Valerie was like.

BARBARA: Will you let mammy decide.

BARRY: Thick as thieves the two of them – and delighted that everyone was intimidated by them.

BARBARA: And Cormac, would you, for Christ sake, stop grinding your teeth!

CORMAC: Sorry, honey.

BARBARA: *(KINDLY)* Just tell us, mammy, which you'd prefer and we'll make the phone-call.

(PAUSE)

ALICE: *(QUIETLY)* Can I maybe have a few minutes alone?

BARBARA: Oh mammy, of course you can.

CORMAC: Absolutely, mother. *(STANDS)*

BARRY: You have a good think, ma. *(STANDS)*

SANDY: Lovely to hear her talk. *(STANDS)*

BARBARA: And take as long as you like – we won't be far.

BARRY: Sandy and I will be upstairs.

BARBARA: Oh for Christ sake!

BARRY: Just to look around!

CORMAC: Yeah, I'd like to look around upstairs too.

BARRY: *(ANNOYED. TO CORMAC)* Would you! So do you want to go first – before me and Sandy or after us?

BARBARA: Mammy, Cormac and I will be in the front-room – we might look at the old photo-album if you don't mind.

CORMAC: Oh right, sure – Sandy, we'll be in the front-room.

SANDY: Barry, we could be in there too, looking at the photo-album.

BARRY: We're going upstairs – come on.

SANDY: We're going upstairs, Cormac.

CORMAC: Okay, Sandy.

BARBARA: Come on, Cormac.

BARRY: *(PAUSING)* Hey, how'll we all know when to come back?

BARBARA: *(COLDLY)* We'll wake you up.

BARRY: Very smart.

(BARRY AND SANDY GO)

BARBARA: You just give us a call, mother.

CORMAC: *(TO ALICE, QUIETLY)* The one with the squirrels.

BARBARA: *(ANGRILY)* Rabbits!

(BARBARA AND CORMAC GO. THEY CLOSE THE KITCHEN DOOR.

ALICE GOES TO THE KITCHEN DOOR AND LOCKS IT. SHE THEN LOCKS THE BACK DOOR. AS IN A PRE-ARRANGED PLAN, SHE PLACES ROLLED-UP RUGS AT THE BOTTOM THE DOORS. THEN SHE TURNS ON THE GAS – ALL JETS. IT HISSES. SHE TAKES THE COSY FROM THE PHONE AND THEN THE PHONE FROM ITS CRADLE. SHE SITS INTO HER CHAIR AND, WITH A LAST DE-CISION, SHE HOLDS THE COSY LOVINGLY ... AND THEN BEGINS TO BREATHE HEAVILY.

41

AS SHE BREATHES IN THE GAS, JIMMY AP-
PEARS AT THE BACK WINDOW. [HE IS NOT IN
THE 'LIGHT' OF ALICE'S MEMORY, BUT IN THE
OUTSIDE RAIN, IN REALITY] HE NOW GOES TO
THE BACK DOOR. HE TRIES TO OPEN IT. THEN
KNOCKS. ALICE DOESN'T HEAR. HE RETURNS
TO THE WINDOW. LOOKS IN. KNOCKS. ALICE
DOESN'T MOVE. HE TURNS TO GO. TURNS BACK
AND KNOCKS AGAIN, NOW LOUDER.

ALICE SUDDENLY HEARS HIM, SITS UP AND
SEES HIM LOOKING IN AT HER)

ALICE: Jimmy! *(TO HERSELF)* Oh my God, this is dreadful.
JIMMY: *(OUTSIDE)* Were you asleep?
ALICE: *(NOW ON HER FEET)* What? Oh yes ...
JIMMY: Sorry for waking you up ...
ALICE: That's all right. *(SHE STOPS. TO HERSELF)* God, the
            gas. *(TO JIMMY)* Jimmy, wait till I open the window.
JIMMY: I can't get in through the window.
ALICE: No, not for you. *(THEN)* Jimmy are there black-
            currants on that bush already?
JIMMY: What?
ALICE: Go over and see if my blackcurrants are coming out.
JIMMY: Blackcurrants? It's raining, Alice.
ALICE: Just see ... *(TO HERSELF)* before I collapse.
JIMMY: Do you know, Alice, there's an old saying about black-
            currants ....
ALICE: Just look at them. Thanks, Jimmy.
JIMMY: Right you are. *(GOES)*
ALICE: *(TO HERSELF)* Don't breathe.
            (SHE TURNS OFF THE GAS AND OPENS THE
            WINDOW – BREATHING IN. PULLS THE RUGS
            FROM THE DOORS. SHE REPLACES THE TELE-
            PHONE, PUTS THE COSY OVER IT AND NOW
            TAKES AN AIR-SPRAY FROM THE TALL UTILITY
            PRESS AND QUICKLY SPRAYS THE ROOM, DIS-
            PLACING THE GAS.

            SUDDEN LOUD KNOCKING ON THE KITCHEN
            DOOR AND THE HANDLE TURNS ANXIOUSLY)
BARBARA: *(OUTSIDE)* Mammy, why is this door locked?
ALICE: Oh Barbara – I'll unlock it now.

	(JIMMY APPEARS AT THE WINDOW. HE IS WET)
JIMMY:	Alice, there *are* blackcurrants but they're still green.
ALICE:	Jimmy, you'll have to go.
JIMMY:	I can't hear you, Alice.
BARBARA:	*(TURNING THE DOOR HANDLE)* Mammy, are you all right?
ALICE:	*(TO JIMMY)* You'll have to go.
BARBARA:	*(OUTSIDE)* Mammy.
JIMMY:	It's the hearing-aid – the rain got on it.
ALICE:	All right, Barbara, I'm coming. *(OPENS THE DOOR TO JIMMY)* Jimmy, could you come back later?
JIMMY:	*(COMING IN)* Why, is there something wrong? *(DOGS ARE HEARD BARKING IN THE DISTANCE)*
ALICE:	*(TO JIMMY)* They're all still here.
JIMMY:	Oh jingos ... *(TURNS TO GO)*
BARBARA:	*(OUTSIDE)* Mammy, Cormac is coming round the back.
ALICE:	*(HOLDS JIMMY'S ARM)* Oh God, Cormac's coming round the back.
JIMMY:	Who?
ALICE:	*(TO JIMMY)* Quick, you'll have to come in and meet them.
JIMMY:	Oh no, they don't like me ... they hate me ...
ALICE:	*(PULLS HIM IN)* Come in or Cormac will see you – hide, I'll get rid of them. *(AS JIMMY THINKS OF GETTING UNDER THE TABLE)* Not there, they'll see you – quick, into the press.
JIMMY:	*(STOPS)* Is your gas on, Alice?
ALICE:	*(ANXIOUSLY PULLS HIM)* Here, stand in here – Cormac is coming, there's the dogs. *(JIMMY STANDS IN THE TALL UTILITY PRESS THAT HOLDS MOPS, PROVISIONS, PAPER TOWELS AND CUTLERY)*
BARBARA:	*(RATTLING THE DOOR)* Mammy.
ALICE:	I'll say I need more time to think then I'll let you out. *(SHE CLOSES THE PRESS DOOR)* Coming Barbara. *(THE PRESS DOOR OPENS – JIMMY ABOUT TO ASK A QUESTION. ALICE SLAMS IT AND QUICK-LY UNLOCKS THE DOOR FOR BARBARA ... AND RETREATS)*

BARBARA: Mammy, are you all right?

ALICE: *(EXHAUSTED)* I'm grand.

BARBARA: What happened? Why was the door locked?

ALICE: I wanted to think in peace.

BARBARA: And what's that smell? Is that an aerosol?

ALICE: Oh yes – it was getting stuffy – I opened the doors and windows as well.

BARBARA: *(TAKES THE AEROSOL)* I'll put that away.

ALICE: Thanks.

(AS BARBARA IS ABOUT TO OPEN THE PRESS DOOR, ALICE REALISES AND SNAPS THE AEROSOL BACK)

ALICE: No, I'll put it away.

BARBARA: *(CLOSING THE WINDOW)* And who were you talking to?

(ALICE QUICKLY OPENS THE PRESS DOOR, JIMMY'S HAND APPEARS AND ALICE GIVES HIM THE AEROSOL AND CLOSES THE DOOR. ALL AS)

ALICE: I wasn't talking to anyone.

BARBARA: Mammy, I heard you talking.

ALICE: You complain when I don't talk and you complain when I do.

BARBARA: I don't complain unless you're talking to yourself – you really do need looking-after.

ALICE: Yes and I wonder could I have more time to ...

BARBARA: No, mammy – I'm sorry but if you haven't made your decision by now we may have to decide for you.

ALICE: Yes but if you could give me five minutes on my own ...

BARBARA: No, mammy – we have to go to Donegal and ...

ALICE: Just five minutes, Barbara.

(THE KITCHEN DOOR OPENS. BARRY COMES IN. HE IS WITHOUT HIS JACKET AND HIS SHIRT IS PARTLY OUTSIDE HIS TROUSERS. SANDY FOLLOWS, LOOKING A LITTLE DISHEVELLED)

BARRY: What's all the shouting about?

BARBARA: Barry! Please dress yourself.

BARRY: *(PUSHES HIS SHIRT IN)* What? Oh right. Sandy heard someone screaming ...

BARBARA: Mammy had locked herself in here and was talking

	to herself – but now she's going to make up her mind.
BARRY:	Is there a funny smell in here?
BARBARA:	She was aerosolling when she should have been deciding.
	(CORMAC COMES IN THE BACK DOOR. HE IS WET. THE DOGS ARE STILL BARKING IN THE DISTANCE)
CORMAC:	Ah, there she is.
BARBARA:	What the hell kept you, Cormac?
CORMAC:	Damn dogs wouldn't leave me alone – is she okay?
BARBARA:	She's fine – she locked the door to make up her mind and now she is going to give us her answer.
CORMAC:	Great. Hey, what's that weird smell?
BARBARA:	Cormac, can we for Christ sake first get this sorted out, unless you want me to be worried sick in Donegal as well?!
CORMAC:	No, honey, I certainly don't.
BARBARA:	Good. So mammy, what's your answer?
	(SILENCE. THEN THE PHONE RINGS, UNDER THE COSY)
ALICE:	Ah there's my telephone.
BARBARA:	Leave it, leave it ...
BARRY:	I'll get it ...
BARBARA:	Just take a message – we're wasting no more time.
BARRY:	Will do. *(INTO PHONE)* Hello?
BARBARA:	Cormac, have the brochures ready.
BARRY:	*(INTO PHONE)* Yes it is Barry.
BARBARA:	*(ANGRILY)* For Christ sake, Barry, take a message – and let's do this now!
CORMAC:	Barbara, will you for God's sake calm down.
BARBARA:	Don't tell me to calm down!
CORMAC:	There's no sense in getting bloody hysterical.
BARBARA:	*(ANGRILY)* Okay, I won't get bloody hysterical, I'll wait till you get bloody hysterical the next time you can't get work and I'm working my ass off doing even more overtime ...
CORMAC:	I get work, I get work!
BARBARA:	Enough for all the trips home, for the car, for the apartment ...? Barry, what the hell are you at there?
BARRY:	*(INTO PHONE)* For God's sake, stop talking rubbish,

	Valerie.
BARBARA:	Valerie?
ALICE:	Ah it's Valerie – to wish me a Happy ...
BARBARA:	Leave her – Barry will phone her back.
SANDY:	Barry, will not phone her back!
BARBARA:	Don't you contradict me!
SANDY:	Barry, are you talking to your wife?
BARRY:	*(TO SANDY)* It's all right, love.
SANDY:	It's not all right – you said you wouldn't talk to her or see her or ...
BARBARA:	Oh for God's sake – not this!
BARRY:	*(INTO THE PHONE)* Yes she is here and don't you call her that.
SANDY:	Call me what? What did she call me? Barry, what did she call me?
BARBARA:	*(TO SANDY)* Will you keep your voice down.
BARRY:	*(INTO PHONE)* Well you're wrong – as a matter of fact she turns me on every time.
SANDY:	*(FURIOUS)* Stop it, Barry, stop talking about me like that!
	(SANDY SLAMS HER FIST ONTO THE TABLE SPILLING A CUP OF TEA)
BARBARA:	For God's sake control yourself – where's the kitchen towels? *(LOOKS UNDER THE SINK)*
BARRY:	*(ANGRILY INTO THE PHONE)* Don't kid yourself, Valerie – you couldn't turn on an electric light.
SANDY:	I'm not taking this! Get off that phone, Barry!
BARBARA:	*(TO ALICE)* Where are your kitchen towels? *(NO REPLY AND SHE GOES TO THE UTILITY PRESS)*
ALICE:	*(REALISES TOO LATE)* No ...
BARBARA:	*(GOES TO THE PRESS WHERE JIMMY IS)* Kitchen towels – and will everyone please shut-up and ...!
ALICE:	No, Barbara. Don't open that ...
	(BARBARA HAS OPENED THE PRESS. JIMMY IS STANDING THERE. JIMMY HANDS HER A ROLL OF KITCHEN TOWEL. SHE SEEMS TO THANK HIM – THEN SUDDENLY REALISES, SCREAMS AND JUMPS BACK. SANDY SEES HIM AND ALSO SCREAMS)
BARRY:	*(SLAMS THE PHONE DOWN)* Jesus Christ!

CORMAC: Who's that!
           *(JIMMY FEARFULLY STEPS OUT. CORMAC GRABS
           A LONG KNIFE)*
CORMAC: Okay, buddy, that's far enough ...
BARRY: Sandy, will you shut shaggin' up.
CORMAC: *(AGGRESSIVELY)* Get your hands up, buddy, or you
           are dead meat.
ALICE: He mightn't be able to hear you because the rain got
           on his hearing-aid.
CORMAC: What?
BARBARA: *(REALISES)* That's old Heffernan, isn't it?
BARRY: It's old Mad Heffernan.
CORMAC: It *is* Mad Heffernan.
BARBARA: What's he doing in there, mammy?
ALICE: Mr Heffernan came for my birthday.
BARRY: You knew he was here?
ALICE: I let him in.
BARBARA: And how long has he been skulking in there?
ALICE: He only arrived.
BARRY: And you were hiding him?
SANDY: Barry, is he deaf and dumb?
BARBARA: So this is who you were talking to.
ALICE: Mr Heffernan is a great friend of mine, Barbara.
BARBARA: *(ANGRILY)* He most certainly is not a friend of yours,
           mammy, or of this family ...
ALICE: He is, Barbara.
BARRY: He's a mad bastard ...
BARBARA: Mammy, we never let him near this house – or have
           you forgotten how our daddy died?
BARRY: And that was the bastard who was responsible for
           him dying ...
ALICE: Oh no, Barry ...
BARBARA: Mammy, everybody knows what that man did ...
ALICE: He did nothing ...
BARRY: Nothing? He saw daddy going into the field ...
ALICE: Barry!
BARBARA: Yes mammy – and he locked the gate and let the bull
           get at daddy and pretended he didn't hear daddy
           screaming, being gored by that bull for a full fifteen
           minutes ...

BARRY:	... while he sat outside the gate ...
BARBARA:	... eating daddy's cheese-sandwiches ...
SANDY:	His cheese sandwiches?
BARRY:	The bastard was eating his sandwiches while daddy was kicking and screaming and clawing at the other side of the gate with the bull on top of him and the big horns twisting in and out of him and the blood pumping up onto the gate ...
ALICE:	Barry, stop!
BARRY:	No ma – and the police knew he was to blame but he knew they couldn't prove it ...
ALICE:	Barry, you stop this at once – you weren't even born when your father was ...
BARRY:	Doesn't matter – the whole town knew it.
BARBARA:	And then, mammy, worst of all, he took daddy's van and drove it around the town, smirking at us as is he did nothing – but we knew he did it and why he did it.
JIMMY:	*(ANGRILY)* I never did anything – my hearing-aid was turned off so I couldn't hear anything ....
BARRY:	Liar – not only are you a liar but you are a murderer and everybody in this town knows all about you and your mad ways and the ways of your wife, Mad Mona, putting smiles on the corpses down at the funeral home.
ALICE:	*(SUDDENLY ANGRY)* Barry, don't you dare speak to Mr Heffernan like that.
BARRY:	I will because it's all bloody true.
ALICE:	It is not – and you have some respect: he is old enough to be your father ...
BARRY:	I never had a father, thanks to him.
ALICE:	*(ANGRILY)* Well I'm telling you now that he could be your father, so show some respect. *(POINTED)* Think of who you are talking to.
BARRY:	*(STOPS)* What?
ALICE:	*(ANGRILY)* You heard me, you heard what I said.
BARBARA:	Mammy what are you going on about now?
ALICE:	And you heard me too, Barbara. Now.
BARRY:	*(QUIETLY. ANXIOUSLY)* Wait a minute – Barbara, I was born nine months after daddy ...

BARBARA:	*(DISMISSIVE)* For God's sake, Barry!
BARRY:	Ma, you ... you're not now telling me that ...
ALICE:	I said what I said – that he could be, Barry, *could* be your father – so show some respect ...
JIMMY:	*(ANXIOUSLY)* Alice, can I talk to you?
ALICE:	No Jimmy.
BARBARA:	Now mammy, you listen to me: I don't know what this is all about and who's Barry's father and who isn't and frankly I don't really care ...
BARRY:	Well, I shaggin care!
BARBARA:	... because I am determined not to be side-tracked again this year into some game to avoid the real issue of you choosing which nursing home
ALICE:	I know, Barbara, and I have been thinking over what you've been saying and I think I should be sensible, so I've made my decision as to where I'll go.
BARBARA:	*(RELIEVED)* Oh mammy, that's great, that's all we wanted. And it's all for your own good – you'll be looked after in case you fall or hurt yourself or ...
CORMAC:	... and, mother, we can be quite confident in recommending either of the homes ...
ALICE:	So my decision is that I'm going ... nowhere. I'm staying here in my own house.
CORMAC:	What?
BARBARA:	But mammy, you can't – you can't be left on your own – we'd be worried sick if you were left on your own for another twelve months ...
ALICE:	But I won't be on my own because ... *(DECIDES)* because Jimmy and his wife Mona are going to look after me – that's what he came to tell me – didn't you, Jimmy *(LOUDLY)* You came to say you're going to look after me.
JIMMY:	*(UNSURE)* Why, where are you going, Alice?
ALICE:	Jimmy, will you listen! – I'm staying here and you're looking after me, you and Mona – isn't that what you were telling me?
JIMMY:	*(REALISES)* Oh that's right.
SANDY:	Ah lovely – my granny has an old chap who ...
BARBARA:	*(SEETHING)* Mammy, is that your final word?
BARRY:	It can't be.

ALICE: And maybe next year, after I see how it goes, I'll go to one of the homes.

BARRY: *(LOUDLY)* For Christ sake are you saying that Mad Heffernan is going to be in this house ...?

ALICE: *(LOUDLY)* Barry, don't use that kind of language in front of two people who could be your parents.

BARRY: What? *(ANXIOUSLY)* Barbara?

BARBARA: *(TO ALICE)* So what you're telling us now is that we're to go home and wait and worry and postpone our lives for another year before you move out of this place?

ALICE: *(CASUALLY)* And next year I'll probably go to Daffy-down-dilly or ...

BARBARA: Right! That's it! Cormac, we are going ...

CORMAC: Where?

BARBARA: To Donegal, where even the sheep will probably show more common sense. And mammy, all right, you can have your way this year – but be it on your head what happens to you and what happens to me, worried sick about you for another twelve months ...

BARRY: And me – do you think I'm not worried?

ALICE: It's only a year ...

BARBARA: Have you everything, Cormac?

CORMAC: *(WITH HIS CAMERA)* Yes – and maybe a photo of ...

BARBARA: Don't take a photograph of that man in this house where he should never be! I presume, Mr Heffernan, we will not see you next year. Kiss Mammy, Cormac.

CORMAC: *(KISSES ALICE)* If you change your mind, phone us in Donegal.

BARBARA: Goodbye Barry – safe journey and all that.

BARRY: *(CONCERNED)* Listen, Barbara, do you think there's anything in what she said about ...
(AS CORMAC TAKES A 'POSED' PHOTO OF SANDY)

BARBARA: *(HARD TO BARRY)* And would you, for Christ sake, between now and next year, start acting your age. *(GOING)* Come on, Cormac – I'll phone you from Donegal, mammy.

CORMAC: See you, Sandy – *(HANDS HER HIS CARD)* ... if you ever ...

BARBARA:	Cormac, come on!
CORMAC:	*(TAKES BACK THE CARD, NERVOUSLY)* Sure, honey.
BARBARA:	And stop grinding your teeth. *(SNAPS THE CARD FROM CORMAC AND TEARS IT. BARBARA AND CORMAC LEAVE)*
BARRY:	We'll be off too, ma – sorry it's only a dash ...
ALICE:	That's all right, Barry – and give that child something to eat.
SANDY:	I'm not hungry, really.
BARRY:	I will, ma. *(STOPS)* And ma, listen, can I ask you something, privately?
ALICE:	This is private enough – go on, Barry.
BARRY:	Well ... *(NOTICES JIMMY LISTENING. GIVES UP)* Nothing. See you next year.
ALICE:	Yes – and maybe then I'll go into Chestnut Downs.
BARRY:	Yeah. *(LOOKS AT JIMMY)* Oh Christ! *(GOES)*
SANDY:	Goodbye. *(TO JIMMY)* Maybe see you next year.
BARRY:	*(OFF)* Come on, Sandy.
SANDY:	Coming.
	(SANDY GOES QUICKLY)
ALICE:	Now, wasn't that a close one – but safe for another twelve months, thanks be to God.
JIMMY:	Alice ...?
ALICE:	And you being here gave me the strength, Jimmy – and that fella with the knife – I'd've told them you were a soldier on D-day, massacring Germans.
JIMMY:	Alice can I ask you ...
ALICE:	And look, left me all the washing up – she'll be on the phone from Donegal, I don't mind that – but next year they'll all be back with a vengeance, intent on putting me in among them cross nurses and a crowd of slobbering oul wans and oul fellas, spilling their food and wetting their beds when they're not all sitting around in their slippers, looking out the window, with their false teeth in their pockets. Well please God I won't have to come to that.
JIMMY:	Alice, I've been wondering about what you said to Barry.
ALICE:	What was that?

51

JIMMY:	Well, how I could be his ... father.
ALICE:	Ah Jimmy, there was only one Immaculate Conception.
JIMMY:	Aye, but the night Walter died ...
ALICE:	What about it?
JIMMY:	Well, it never crossed my mind before ... I thought I knew it couldn't possibly be ... but now I've been counting backwards and, remember, I came to console you after the funeral and I had a bottle of whiskey and ...
ALICE:	That's right and you gave me a hug, Jimmy ...
JIMMY:	Ah no, Alice, I had a bottle and what's this happened? – yes, you were terrible upset and I ...
ALICE:	You gave me a hug ....
JIMMY:	... and we had a little drink and I ... fell asleep then – that's right, that's all it was – but then when you said to Barry I began to wonder ...
ALICE:	Jimmy, will you stop – do you think I would have said it if it was true?
JIMMY:	What?
ALICE:	That was just to stop him in his tracks, and it did – and, Jimmy Heffernan, if you start saying anything else now, I'll only get annoyed with you and have to send you home to Mona, birthday or no birthday ...
JIMMY:	So you're sure?
ALICE:	There's nothing to be sure about. Now give me a hand here.
JIMMY:	Right. *(HELPING HER)* And me and Mona will drop over to see you from time to time.
	(ALREADY WE CAN HEAR THE RECORD OF 'BUBBLES' PLAYING UNDER, AS)
ALICE:	Course you will. You get on well together, don't you: you and Mona.
JIMMY:	Oh we do – though there's always things I wish for, Alice.
ALICE:	We all wish for things, Jimmy – but at least I know I have another year under my own roof anyway.
JIMMY:	Yes. *(SADLY)* And I have Mona.

(ALICE LOOKS PUZZLED AT JIMMY. WE HOLD.

52

THE MUSIC IS LOUDER AS THE LIGHTS FADE TO BLACK)

END OF ACT ONE

ACT TWO
ONE YEAR LATER

SOME MONTHS HAVE PASSED. ALICE'S KITCHEN, AS BE-
FORE. A TABLE WITH BOTTLES AND GLASSES. WE HEAR THE
TINKLING PIANO PLAYING 'BUBBLES', SOFTLY. THE WEAT-
HER OUTSIDE IS DULL.

ALICE IS ON A STEP-LADDER AT THE WINDOW, WITH A
HACK-SAW, CUTTING ONE OF THE BARS. SHE QUIETLY
SINGS TO THE MUSIC. JIMMY APPEARS AT THE BACK DOOR.
HE OPENS IT, COMES IN – NOT SEEING ALICE AND SHE NOT
SEEING HIM.

JIMMY: Alice?

ALICE: *(IN FRIGHT)* My God! *(CALLS)* Up here, Jimmy.

JIMMY: *(NOT HEARING. TOWARDS THE KITCHEN DOOR)* Alice, are you there?

ALICE: Up here, Jimmy. *(HE SEES HER AS SHE COMES DOWN)* I'm thinking of taking down the bars.

JIMMY: What jars?

ALICE: The bars, Jimmy.

JIMMY: *(ANGRILY ADJUSTS HIS HEARING AID)* Cursed batteries the cause of it all ...!

ALICE: *(LOUDLY)* The people that moved in next door, he's a policeman and he said they were dangerous. Have you a hack-saw yourself, Jimmy? – this wouldn't cut butter.

JIMMY: Mona is gone, Alice.

ALICE: Gone where, Jimmy?

JIMMY: She's passed on, Alice – she's dead, laid out down in the hospital.

ALICE: Oh merciful God, Jimmy – sit down there, let me get you a cup of tea.

JIMMY: No no, I'm on my way now to make the arrange-ments ...

ALICE: But when did this happen – was she knocked down or ...?

JIMMY: Just last night, in the kitchen, she came back from laying-out poor Mrs Williamson ...

ALICE: Lord have mercy on her too ...

JIMMY: ... and she must have got up on that chair to wind the
            kitchen clock and lost her balance and fell and crack-
            ed her head on the stone floor and maybe she was
            shouting for me ...

ALICE: You weren't there?

JIMMY: I went off to bed because I had an early start today ...

ALICE: So it was only this morning you ...?

JIMMY: Oh no, I missed her coming to bed – Mona always leps
            into the bed ... and I'm always telling her it's a bed
            not a trampoline ... *(THEN)* ... I mean, she *used* to al-
            ways lep into the bed ...

ALICE: I know, Jimmy ...

JIMMY: Always wakening me up and last night when she
            didn't wake me up lepping in, that's what woke me
            up ... and I looked at the clock and it was nearly one,
            so down I came because I'd left out her milk and bis-
            cuits like I always do if I go off first ... and there she
            was on the floor ... and the clock there and the chair
            overturned – that same chair I was intending to fix
            because the legs were shaky ...

ALICE: And was she ...?

JIMMY: Oh I knew she was gone. In Normandy, I used to see
            the soldiers dying and dead so I knew ...

ALICE: You should have phoned me, Jimmy ...

JIMMY: And she was in great form going out – looking for-
            ward to laying-out Mrs Williamson – and just today,
            Mr Williamson said she done a great job, the best she
            ever done.

ALICE: She always did a great job.

JIMMY: But who'll be laying out Mona, down in that place?

ALICE: At the hospital, did you say?

JIMMY: Yes, a post mortem because she wasn't sick a day in
            her life – laid out on a slab.

ALICE: Sure as soon as they're done, they'll have her home
            again.

JIMMY: They're the arrangements I'm going to make now.

ALICE: Jimmy, is there anything I can do?

JIMMY: There's nothing anyone can do, Alice. *(THEN)* But
            maybe tomorrow, after it's all over, I might drop over
            ...

55

ALICE:	Do, of course.
JIMMY:	There's only the two nephews that'll be up and they won't stay long.
ALICE:	Then you come over immediately they're gone.
JIMMY:	That's the saddest time. And I must do them bars for you sometime ... and I was thinking, you should get rid of that gas, that's too much of a temptation.
ALICE:	The gas is grand, Jimmy.
JIMMY:	*(ANNOYED)* The last thing we want now is another death.
ALICE:	*(WEAKLY)* What?
JIMMY:	And doing them bars will keep my mind off other things. Bloody hearing-aid is working perfect now.
ALICE:	Now, you mustn't blame yourself, Jimmy.
JIMMY:	I do, Alice. *(GOING)* It'll be a long day before I forget this.
	(JIMMY GOES. ALICE PUTS THE HACK-SAW INTO THE KITCHEN DRAWER. GUILTILY TURNS THE GAS ON AND OFF. GOES TO HER EASY CHAIR AND SITS. SUDDENLY THE KITCHEN DOOR IS OPENED AND BARRY STEPS IN. HE LOOKS MORE THAN A YEAR OLDER – HIS HAIR GREYING. HE NOW SMOKES CHEROOTS)
BARRY:	Ma, we've arrived – Happy Birthday!
	(SUDDENLY EVERYTHING CHANGES. THE BARS DISAPPEAR FROM THE WINDOW, THE DULL WEATHER OUTSIDE TURNS TO BRIGHT SUN-SHINE. THE MUSIC STOPS. BARRY IS IN AND HUGGING ALICE, ALL NON-STOP ENTHUSIASM)
BARRY:	Wake up, ma – did we give you a fright?
ALICE:	No, I was just ...
BARRY:	You left the front door open ...
ALICE:	Did I?
BARRY:	Yes you did and Sandy's here, you remember Sandy *(SHOUTS)* Sandy? *(TO ALICE)* Did Barbara arrive yet, did she leave the door open?
ALICE:	No, she's not here yet ...
BARRY:	And today's a big day for you, eh, ma?
ALICE:	Ah yes, another birthday ...
BARRY:	No, today's the day you promised to pick the nursing

	home – haven't forgotten, I hope.
ALICE:	Oh no ...
BARRY:	*(MERRILY SALUTES, TO ATTENTION)* Today, Barbara expects every man to do his duty. *(THEN SHOUTS)* Sandy? Where are you?
ALICE:	*(CONCERNED)* Barry, about the nursing home ...
BARRY:	We were going to bring a birthday cake but then, I thought, Barbara and Cormac will have one ... *(SHOUTS)* Sandy! *(TO ALICE)* ... and on top of that we decided to keep on driving – left Basingstoke at 9am on the M3, onto the North Circular at Junction 12, off at Uxbridge, onto the M40, around Birmingham, switched to the M54 to Telford, Holyhead thirty minutes before the boat left and on arrival at Dun Laoghaire, kept driving all the way here. *(SHOUTS)* Sandy? *(TO ALICE)* And the house looks the same – no, the bars are gone, where are the bars?
ALICE:	Well a policeman moved in next door ...
	(SANDY APPEARS, FLUSTERED. SHE SEEMS MUCH MORE SETTLED, MUCH LESS SEXY OR GLAMOROUS, IN LOOSE-FITTING CLOTHES)
BARRY:	Sandy, where did you get to?
SANDY:	I went to the loo.
BARRY:	*(LIGHTLY)* Before you said Happy Birthday to ma, you went to the loo?
SANDY:	I had to when I wasn't allowed to get out of the car.
BARRY:	You should have asked, sweetheart. *(OF ALICE)* Now, here she is – the Birthday Girl.
SANDY:	*(KISSES ALICE)* Hello, a very happy birthday.
ALICE:	Thank you, Sandy – did you have a nice journey.
SANDY:	Yes, lovely – top speed all the way ...
BARRY:	... couldn't wait to see my old ma – and she hasn't changed at all – has she, Sandy?
SANDY:	No – you're looking more like my old granny.
ALICE:	Oh thanks very much.
SANDY:	No, she's lovely.
BARRY:	But now the big question – have we changed, looking at us now? I know, the grey hair: that's called maturity, ma. And the house has changed a bit. Notice the bars, Sandy.

SANDY:	What bars?
BARRY:	That's what I mean – they're gone.
SANDY:	Oh yes – looks much better that way.
ALICE:	Yes. And is everything all right with you, Sandy?
SANDY:	Pardon?
BARRY:	She couldn't be better, ma, still doing the reflexology, fully qualified now – and I'm happy to say that my sales business is even better: had the second-best sales return this month beating seven English guys – leave it to the Irish every time.
ALICE:	*(TO SANDY)* No, I was just wondering about you because on the phone at Christmas you were telling me about the baby.
SANDY:	Oh yes, well ...
BARRY:	*(ANGRILY TAKES SANDY ASIDE)* I didn't know you told her that?
SANDY:	I just mentioned it.
BARRY:	... after I said nothing about it ...
SANDY:	I didn't know you'd said nothing ...
BARRY:	... course I said nothing because we agreed to say nothing ...
SANDY:	But I thought your mother could be told.
BARRY:	Well yes, sure, you're right, sweetheart. *(TO ALICE)* Sorry ma, I would have mentioned it at Christmas only so many things can go wrong with having a baby and as it happened something did go wrong ...
ALICE:	Ah ...
BARRY:	... and although we managed to get Sandy to the hospital, she lost it on the way ...
ALICE:	Ah dear.
BARRY:	Naturally, we were all very disappointed – but I always say, so many things can go wrong, better to say nothing.
ALICE:	*(TO SANDY)* But you're all right, are you?
SANDY:	Yes I am now, thank you.
BARRY:	*(MERRILY)* And only rearing to get into this birthday party – sing-song, cake, whatever – and then the restaurant is on us – did you tell Barbara the restaurant is on us?
ALICE:	I did and she ...

BARRY:	And no objections considered. And Sandy, the birth-day present. *(TO ALICE)* We picked you a great present this year – how's the coffee-maker, by the way?
ALICE:	The what?
BARRY:	Turns on the radio, pours the cappuccino, wakes you up?
ALICE:	Oh that – I'd be lost without it.
BARRY:	Well wait'll you see what we have for you this year – two presents. Do you want to bring them in, Sandy? *(THROWS THE CAR-KEYS ON THE TABLE)*
SANDY:	Me?
BARRY:	*(SWEETLY)* Well you packed the car, sweetheart – you're the one that said it was your car and you knew how to pack it and unpack it.
SANDY:	Right! *(GOES ANGRILY)*
BARRY:	Great. Sandy's brother, Darren, helped her pack the car. Nice fellow, Darren – drives a juggernaut. *(AWKWARDLY)* And any other news, ma? – apart from what you write ...
ALICE:	Not really, Barry.
BARRY:	So you're ... here on your own, are you? *(LOOKS INTO THE UTILITY PRESS)*
ALICE:	Pardon?
BARRY:	You don't see, what's-his-name, Mr Heffernan, at all?
ALICE:	Ah no.
BARRY:	Right. *(LOOKING OUT)* And the garden looks well. *(THEN)* Very nice flowers. *(ALREADY THE TINKLING PIANO PLAYING 'BUB-BLES' IS HEARD AS THE DAY OUTSIDE DULLS AND JIMMY COMES IN THROUGH THE BACK DOOR. BARRY, WITH LITTLE TO SAY, LOOKS OUT THE WINDOW ... AS ALICE REMEMBERS)*
JIMMY:	The mass-card and the flowers were lovely, Alice.
ALICE:	The least I could do. Poor Mona – it was a lovely funeral. I missed you after.
JIMMY:	You missed the laughter?
ALICE:	No, after – you didn't drop by after the funeral.
JIMMY:	Oh I know – and that's what I'm here to apologise for ...
ALICE:	Not at all – I know that your nephews probably stay-

	ed a few days ...
JIMMY:	No, they galloped off as soon as we got back..
ALICE:	... or that you must have been tired or ...
JIMMY:	No, Alice, it was the police that stayed. *(JIMMY TURNS TO GO)*
ALICE:	The police?!
BARRY:	And Valerie, do you ever see Valerie?
	(THE MUSIC STOPS, THE LIGHTS CHANGE QUICKLY TO LIGHT OUTSIDE, JIMMY IS GONE AS ALICE IS JOLTED BACK TO THE PRESENT)
ALICE:	Sorry, Barry, I didn't quite hear ...
BARRY:	I was wondering if you ever see Valerie?
ALICE:	Valerie? Oh yes, occasionally, and my grandchildren.
BARRY:	Yeah, they're keeping well – I phoned her once or twice ...
ALICE:	Yes, she said you rang her.
BARRY:	Oh yes, we keep in touch ... well, why not. *(GOES TO THE PHONE)* In fact, ma, I might phone her now from here, just to say I've arrived – I meant to do it, but Sandy ... you wouldn't mind ...?
	(BARRY HAS ALREADY LIFTED THE COSY FROM THE PHONE – WHEN BARBARA COMES IN. SHE CARRIES A CAKE. SHE HAS A CIGARETTE IN HER MOUTH AND SEEMS EVEN MORE TENSE THAN LAST YEAR)
BARBARA:	Mammy! Oh mammy, mammy, mammy!
	(SHE VIGOROUSLY HUGS ALICE)
ALICE:	Barbara! I thought you'd be here earlier ...
BARBARA:	The flight was routed through London – Cormac made the reservation. Barry! – you're gone grey!
BARRY:	That's called maturity, Barbara. *(TO ALICE)* I told you she'd bring the cake.
BARBARA:	Really organised this year – did I interrupt you on the phone ...?
BARRY:	No. *(REALISES THAT HE IS HOLDING THE COSY)* I was just looking at it.
BARBARA:	*(LAUGHS)* Do they not have phones in Basingstoke?
BARRY:	*(TOLERANTLY)* Very good. *(REPLACES THE COSY)*
BARBARA:	And is that Mandy I saw unpacking your car onto the sidewalk?

BARRY: Sandy – she's getting our presents for ma.

BARBARA: (TO ALICE) And we have something very special for you, mammy – something for the future.

ALICE: You shouldn't be bothering ...

BARBARA: Not at all – Cormac has it. (CHEERFULLY) And talking of the future, I think we should all have our little chat, make all our arrangements, sooner than later this year ...

BARRY: And the restaurant is on us, Barbara ...

BARBARA: Sure, but that comes after we have finalised everything – then we can enjoy ourselves.
(DOGS ARE HEARD BARKING OUTSIDE)

BARRY: Ma says she's all set to pick her nursing home.

ALICE: (CONCERNED) No I ...

BARBARA: I know she is   she promised me at Christmas, didn't you, mammy? Now, I'll have some of that brandy – this jet-lag is hitting me already.

BARRY: Is Cormac not with you?

ALICE: (HEARING THE DOGS) I think he's coming around the back.

BARBARA: He is, mammy – how did you know? – it was to be a surprise, to catch us in conversation. Cormac has been amazingly successful this last year – he is now full-time and he couldn't be happier.

BARRY: Full-time at what?

BARBARA: Photo-news reporting, what he always wanted to do, why we went to America in the first place – he's had his video on CNN. (TO ALICE) That's a huge television station, mammy.

BARRY: His video of what?

BARBARA: I'll let him tell you – but do you remember that video of the police beating up Rodney King in Los Angeles – ah, here he is ...
(CORMAC BURSTS IN THE BACK DOOR. HE CARRIES A LARGE FILM CAMERA ON HIS SHOULDER [SLIGHTLY OUTDATED IN ITS SIZE] WITH A FIXED LIGHT, NOW DAZZLING EVERYBODY. HE IS DRESSED IN HIS PERCEPTION OF HOW MEDIA PEOPLE SHOULD LOOK. THE DOGS ARE STILL BARKING. HE IS FILMING AS HE ENTERS)

ALICE: Ah hello, Cormac.

BARRY: Hello Cormac.

CORMAC: Just keep talking, folks.

BARBARA: Come in, honey – I was just telling everybody about your triumphs.

CORMAC: No honey, chat between yourselves. *(POSITIONS HIMSELF IN FRONT OF ALICE AND BARBARA)*

BARBARA: *(POSING FOR THE CAMERA)* All right. *(TO ALICE)* Hello Mammy, how are you?

ALICE: *(LOST)* Pardon?

BARBARA: *(TO ALICE)* And who's birthday is it today?

ALICE: *(LOST)* Pardon?

BARBARA: *(STERNLY)* All right that's enough, Cormac, put it down now, you're blinding us all – and wish mammy a happy birthday.

CORMAC: Okay, sure. I'll get you all later. *(SWITCHES OFF THE CAMERA LIGHT)* Mother, Happy Birthday to you. *(KISSES HER)*

ALICE: Thank you, Cormac.

CORMAC: That dog is new, isn't he?

ALICE: He belongs next door – he's a policeman.

CORMAC: *(SWITCHES ON THE CAMERA LIGHT)* The dog's a police dog – my God, get some footage.

ALICE: *(CONTROLLED)* No, the man's a policeman – the dog is just a dog!

CORMAC: Ah, thought there could be a story – we stay on the ball in my business. *(SWITCHES OFF THE LIGHT AGAIN)* Oh hi, Barry – saw Sandy outside, got some footage of her unloading your car.

BARRY: Great. And you're big into news reporting now?

CORMAC: Got the big break, Barry – been on CNN. *(LOUDLY TO ALICE)* That's a TV station, mother.

BARBARA: I told her all that.

CORMAC: *(TO BARBARA)* About Rodney King?

BARBARA: No, honey, I didn't tell her that.

BARRY: But you didn't film Rodney King – wasn't Rodney King filmed by a black guy who ...

CORMAC: Yeah sure, but I got down there and filmed those closest to him.

BARRY: To Rodney King?

CORMAC: No, the guy who filmed Rodney King and sold it to CNN. Big time, buddy – I got my freelance card and two weeks later I kissed all the bitty work goodbye, invested 3,000 dollars in equipment and started rolling. Now I miss nothing – to me, everything is news.

BARBARA: A lady got sick on the plane and Cormac filmed her from beginning to end.

CORMAC: See, if she'd died that would have been news.

BARRY: And did she die?

CORMAC: No, she was just drunk – but I did get a guy dying in San Francisco ...

BARBARA: ... Yes and that should have been on CNN ...

CORMAC: ... The problem was another camera-man ...

BARBARA: ... as soon as anything happens, all these camera-men swarm in from nowhere ...

CORMAC: ... and this other camera-man got closer and picked up the guy's dying words, which were 'Would someone, for Christ sake, help me' – and if I had got that, my film *would* have been on CNN.

BARBARA: Exactly. And everything is all right with you, mammy? You are looking a little tired ... I think that more than ever, you need looking-after now – and this year we have plenty of time to decide where.

BARRY: She took the bars off the window.

CORMAC: So you did – must get that. *(FILMS THE WINDOW, WITH COMMENTARY)* Take One – Action! 'No bars on the windows anymore.'

BARRY: She left the hall-door open and didn't know it ...

BARBARA: Ah God, mammy – now that's what we worry about.

BARRY: But she never sees what's-his-name Heffernan or anything...

BARBARA: *(TO ALICE)* And we are all very glad of that, mammy, very glad. Here, give me another kiss.

CORMAC: *(FILMING AND DOING THE COMMENTARY)* Take Two – Action! 'Barbara kissing her mother Alice – the occasion of her birthday'. Great sequence that.

BARRY: I'll go and get Sandy. *(GOES)*

CORMAC: *(TO BARRY)* Want a hand there, Barry?

BARRY: *(OFF)* No.

63

ALICE: And everything is all right with you, Barbara?

BARBARA: Oh yes, mammy – bit of jet-lag today but, overall, we couldn't be happier, honestly we couldn't, could we, Cormac?

CORMAC: Couldn't be happier, in the land of plenty.

ALICE: But on the telephone at Christmas, you ...

BARBARA: Oh that! I was tired, mammy, I explained that in my letter ...

ALICE: I was worried because I didn't know who you were screaming at.

BARBARA: *(LAUGHS)* Screaming? I wasn't screaming – when was I ever screaming?

CORMAC: You have to remember, mother, that when you phoned, it was early morning in San Francisco.

BARBARA: It was the middle of the night ...

CORMAC: ... and I had just surprised Barbara with my new camera and all my new equipment ...

BARBARA: ... I was just surprised, mammy – I explained all that – and I was laughing at Cormac with all the equipment he had just gone out and spent 3,000 dollars of our savings on ...

CORMAC: In fairness, you weren't laughing, honey ...

BARBARA: I was laughing, Cormac ...

CORMAC: I have it on film, honey ...

BARBARA: *(SUDDENLY SHARP)* I don't give a damn what you have it on, honey – I was laughing – I wrote to mammy that I was laughing and that's what I was doing – laughing.

CORMAC: Sure honey, later you were ... (laughing) ...

BARBARA: *(TO ALICE)* And I should have phoned you back, mammy, I really should – if I thought I had worried you, I would have phoned you back ...

CORMAC: She would, mother – Barbara is always phoning back to apologise.

BARBARA: In fact, Cormac, I think I said I would phone mammy back – didn't I say that?

CORMAC: Yes you did.

BARBARA: But now we need never worry about you worrying again, need we? – from this year, we'll have other people worrying about you. *(TO CORMAC)* Did you

64

bring all the brochures they sent us, Cormac.

CORMAC: All here, honey.

BARBARA: Great. So, after the birthday presents and the cake, we'll let you make your choice of what nursing home you want.

ALICE: *(CONCERNED)* Barbara ...

BARBARA: *(CHEERFULLY)* And what is this I see arriving? *(THE DOOR HAS OPENED. BARRY AND SANDY STRUGGLE IN WITH A LARGE OBJECT, COMPLETELY WRAPPED IN PAPER. IT IS A ROCKING CHAIR, BUT IS NOT IDENTIFIABLE AS SUCH. SANDY ALSO HAS A BOXED PARCEL)*

BARRY: *(STRUGGLING)* This is for you, ma.

SANDY: *(STRUGGLING)* Hope you like it.

CORMAC: This I must get on film ... *(LIGHT ON AND BEGINS TO FILM)* Take One – Action!

ALICE: Ah Barry ...

BARBARA: God, it's big enough – what can it be ...

CORMAC: *(COMMENTARY)* 'We see the first birthday present arriving – great excitement.'

SANDY: It's just something we thought you'd like ...

BARRY: ... and another present we brought back from our summer holidays ...

SANDY: *(STRUGGLING)* In this box here ...

BARRY: Careful, Sandy, don't tear the paper and give the game away ...

CORMAC: *(COMMENTARY)* 'Sandy and Barry having some trouble entering the room ...'

BARBARA: *(ANNOYED)* Cormac, would you switch that off and go and help them.

BARRY: We can manage ...

CORMAC: *(POINTS THE CAMERA AT BARBARA. COMMENTARY)* 'And Barbara getting annoyed because I said that they were having some trouble ...'

BARBARA: *(ROUGHLY PUSHES THE CAMERA ASIDE)* Cormac, will you take that God-damn thing out of my face!

CORMAC: *(ANGRILY)* Hey, that's three thousand dollars worth of camera! *(SWITCHES OFF)*

BARBARA: Don't I know it – now put it down and go and help

them – that poor girl is pregnant.

CORMAC: Oh of course, sure. I forgot. *(GOES TO HELP THEM)*

BARRY: *(ANGRILY STOPS. TO SANDY)* How the hell did she find out?

SANDY: I didn't tell her.

BARRY: *(ANGRILY)* How many others know?

SANDY: I didn't tell her.

BARRY: Read it in the paper, did she?

SANDY: I don't know!

CORMAC: But Barry, it's great news.

BARRY: It's not great news, it's not news at all.

BARBARA: You mean she's not?

BARRY: *(TO BARBARA)* Why, when the hell did she say she was ...?

SANDY: I never said it at all.

BARBARA: If you must know, it was mammy who said it.

BARRY: *(TO ALICE)* What?

ALICE: *(TO BARBARA)* I didn't think you heard me saying it because remember, at Christmas, you were scream-ing when I was telling you.

BARBARA: For God's sake, I've just explained that I wasn't screaming, I was laughing.

BARRY: Laughing? Why is there something funny about me having a baby?

BARBARA: Not laughing at you!

BARRY: At who then? Who else was having a baby?

SANDY: *(SHOUTS)* Will you shut up – you were never hav-ing a baby, I was having a baby and now I'm not hav-ing it and I'm sick of you being ashamed of it and making me feel ashamed of it too!

(SANDY RUNS OUT THE KITCHEN DOOR, IN TEARS. THEN)

BARBARA: For Christ sake, why the hell would I be laughing at you having or not having babies.

CORMAC: Matter of fact, Barry, she was lying in bed laughing at my equipment.

BARRY: *(STOPS)* Your what?

BARBARA: His bloody second-hand camera – and anyway I don't see why you're so defensive about having a baby.

66

BARRY: I'm not defensive – we just decided not to tell any-
           one in case ... (anything happened)
BARBARA: If you were like us, being asked day-in and day-out
           why we *don't* have a baby ...
CORMAC: I always say it's not my fault.
BARBARA: And what's that supposed to mean? – that it's all my
           fault?
CORMAC: No, I just say that to cover myself if the guys ask me
           why ... (I don't have babies)
BARBARA: There's no need to cover yourself because we'll have
           babies when we're ready ...
CORMAC: That's what I'm saying – we'll get down to it as soon
           as ... you say the word.
BARBARA: And when we have them, we damn-well won't be
           defensive about them.
CORMAC: Damn sure we won't. *(TO BARRY)* We'll be proud to
           have our babies – and that's whether Barbara loses
           some of them or not.
BARBARA: For God's sake ...
CORMAC: No, what I mean is ...
BARBARA: *(EXASPERATED)* Can we leave it at that – and get on
           with what we're here to do and fix mammy up in a
           nice nursing home.
ALICE: Barbara, about the nursing home ...
BARBARA: Mammy, do you have any iced water in this house?
ALICE: Just tap water, Barbara – and about the nursing ...
CORMAC: And I might nip out and see how Sandy is – she ap-
           peared quite upset.
BARBARA: You won't need your camera for that.
CORMAC: Right. *(PUTS IT DOWN)*
BARBARA: *(QUIETLY)* And stop grinding your teeth.
CORMAC: Right. *(GOES)*
BARRY: I was not defensive about the baby – we were de-
           lighted about it and I was delighted that Sandy told
           ma, but I didn't want everyone to know in case some-
           thing went wrong and, ma, you simply shouldn't
           have told Barbara.
ALICE: Sorry, Barry.
BARRY: Okay – just as long as you told no one else.
ALICE: I didn't.

67

BARRY:	Okay. And now the presents.
BARBARA:	All right, the presents – and then we come to mammy ...
ALICE:	Barbara, can I just say ...
	(CORMAC COMES IN WITH SANDY)
CORMAC:	Okay folks, relax, it's all okay now.
BARBARA:	You okay, Sandy?
SANDY:	Yes, thank you – I'm so sorry for ... whatever.
CORMAC:	Sure. I told her that we all wanted to get back to why we're here – mother's birthday – and she brightened up at once, didn't you?
BARBARA:	Great, so let's get onto that now ...
SANDY:	Thank you so much, Cormac. Sorry everybody.
BARRY:	You okay, Sandy?
SANDY:	Yes, Barry – and I only said it to your mother.
BARRY;	Sure and it's okay – we've sorted it out now.
SANDY:	I never said it to anyone else.
BARRY:	I know that, love – it's all fixed up now.
SANDY:	And I just wish we didn't have to see all of this as something we are ashamed of.
BARRY:	*(ANNOYED)* I couldn't agree more – we keep it between ourselves and it's fine. Okay?
SANDY:	Yes, Barry. Thanks again, Cormac.
CORMAC:	My pleasure.
BARBARA:	Okay, now that's out of the way, why don't we ...
CORMAC:	You know, it brings me back, helping out like that – like out on a photo-news assignment for CNN, the number of times I've seen the flak flying ...
BARBARA:	*(QUIETLY)* Give me patience.
CORMAC:	... you step in, calm it down, establish a lasting peace. Makes going into the troubled zone worth while.
SANDY:	Cormac was telling me how he's going to be a war correspondent.
BARRY:	*(COLDLY)* Really? What war?
CORMAC:	You name it, Barry – any of the African States, the Middle East, South America – any of the potential hot spots. I just want to be there, bringing the truth on to CNN – like we did with Rodney King.
SANDY:	I love the Americans on CNN – the way they talk, you just have to believe them because they are so calm, so

sincere ...

CORMAC: Well sure we are – like when I was interviewed on CNN ...

SANDY: You were interviewed on CNN?

CORMAC: Oh sure ...

BARRY: I was interviewed on the BBC.

SANDY: I know, darling – when you were drunk at that football match. *(TO CORMAC)* And was this after the Rodney King trial?

CORMAC: I was interviewed twice, once before each trial ...

BARBARA: Cormac, I don't think mammy wants to hear all this ...

CORMAC: Why not, honey?

BARBARA: Because, honey, mammy wants to open her presents and cut her cake and pick out her favourite nursing home – isn't that right, mammy?

ALICE: Ah no, I'll hear about Burger King

BARBARA: It's Rodney King!

ALICE: Whichever one – I'll hear him too.

BARBARA: *(QUIETLY)* Christ!

CORMAC: Dead right, mother, because this is real behind-the-scenes stuff – I go into any club or meet any folk in the States and I know no one who isn't amazed when they hear this ...

SANDY: Well, it's ever-so unique, isn't it.

BARBARA: Okay, make it quick, Cormac, and then, mammy, we'll open your presents ...

BARRY: And I booked the restaurant for seven ...

CORMAC: Okay – so are you listening, mother?

BARBARA: She is. Get on with it, Cormac.

CORMAC: Okay – picture the scene. It is last year – I know there are racial riots in Los Angeles – you stay aware in the media business – so I get down there just two days after the alleged – we always say alleged – beating of Rodney King by the police officers and by sheer luck I can line-up an interview with a school-pal of the uncle of the guy who filmed Rodney King ...
(THE TINKLING PIANO PLAYING 'BUBBLES' IS HEARD, AS ALICE BEGINS TO REMEMBER)

CORMAC: ... and that is some scoop when you realise that there are maybe 1000 guys with video cameras trying to get on CNN ...

(OUTSIDE, IN ALICE'S MEMORY, THE DAY HAS DULLED AND JIMMY HAS COME IN THROUGH THE BACK DOOR. CORMAC'S VOICE FADES FROM HER CONSCIOUSNESS. ALL IN A FREEZE AS ALICE CONTINUES THE MEMORY THAT WAS INTER-RUPTED EARLIER)

ALICE: The police? The police stayed a few days?

JIMMY: As soon as the funeral and the post mortem was over, they nearly took up residence in the house with their questions and going back and forth over the same ground, questioning this, questioning that ...

ALICE: Questioning what, Jimmy?

JIMMY: ... and then off on a tangent about how many Germans I killed on D-Day and if I did hand-to-hand combat and then suddenly asking me, 'Mr Heffernan, did you strike your wife?' and when he asked me that, didn't the cursed batteries in my hearing-aid go off and I thought he said, 'Mr Heffernan did you like your wife' and I shouted at them 'yes yes yes, I did' and the looks on their faces, the big smiles and the paper pushed in front of me to sign until I told them what I meant and then the questions over and over again ...

ALICE: God, that was dreadful, Jimmy.

JIMMY: Mona – that I looked after all my life.

ALICE: Of course you did. And have they gone now, the police?

JIMMY: Deed they haven't, they're coming back – and I'm to keep myself available for questions and the file might be sent to the Director of Public Prosecutions and who drank the milk.

ALICE: Pardon, Jimmy?

JIMMY: Oh they made a big thing out of the milk I left for Mona – when everyone arrived, the glass was empty but it wasn't in her stomach at the post mortem so they said I must have drank it, and maybe I did, I don't know.

ALICE: You don't remember ...?

70

JIMMY: I was too upset to remember – I only remember seeing her lying there and the blood on her head – I could have reached out and drank it and I told them that a hundred times – and they asking me then did I turn off my hearing-aid and look at her dying while I was drinking the milk.

ALICE: Merciful God.

JIMMY: And that's why I didn't come over after the funeral, Alice.

ALICE: Understandably, Jimmy – that was dreadful.

JIMMY: I'll get home now, in case they come for me – to take me God knows where.

ALICE: Oh Jimmy.

JIMMY: But you believe me, Alice, don't you?

ALICE: Well of course I believe you, Jimmy.

JIMMY: And Alice, you don't believe what they were saying about ... *(ANXIOUSLY)* well dragging in about your Walter dying and the bull and me not hearing and eating the cheese-sandwiches and now Mona and the milk and my hearing-aid again ...

ALICE: Ah Jimmy, stop – that never entered my head – merciful God, such a thing to say.

JIMMY: *(CALMED)* Well that's what matters. I'll let you know if anything happens. *(GOING)*

ALICE: Oh do, Jimmy, do.
(JIMMY GOES)

ALICE: *(TO HERSELF)* Such a thing to say: Walter and the bull and the sandwiches and the milk – ah Walter, poor Walter, such a way for you to die – poor, defenceless Walter, who never hurt a fly, and that savage bull on top of you *(DISTRESSED)* Ah God, when I think of it, that bull ... the bull ... *(SHOUTS INTO HER CONSCIOUSNESS)* The bull, the bull ... Walter!
(THE MUSIC SUDDENLY STOPS. IT TURNS BRIGHT OUTSIDE. CORMAC STOPS TALKING AND ALL TURN TO ALICE WHO HAS SHOUTED)

BARBARA: *(ANXIOUSLY)* Mammy, mammy, mammy, wake up! Stop shouting!

BARRY: Are you all right, ma – you shouted.

ALICE: (LOST) The bull got Walter.

BARBARA: It's all right, mammy – don't you be thinking about that now: have you been watching farming programmes again?

ALICE: No ...

BARBARA: Well don't be even thinking about those animals. Sit back now. That's it. (TO THE OTHERS) She thinks about daddy, how he died.

CORMAC: Oh right – that bull.

BARBARA: Don't say the word, Cormac! And don't you be thinking about it, mammy. Put it out of your mind.

CORMAC: You should have been listening to me about CNN.

BARBARA: She fell asleep listening to you and CNN ...

ALICE: It's all fixed up now – nothing to worry about now.

BARBARA: Exactly. So now, let's get on with the birthday and, now, the presents ...

BARRY: Great – and can we go first: we have two presents ...

BARBARA: It doesn't matter who goes first ...

CORMAC: (WITH HIS CAMERA) Get this on film ...

BARRY: Okay, Sandy we'll give her the small one first ... the one you got ...

ALICE: You shouldn't be bothering with presents ...

CORMAC: (COMMENTARY) Take One – Action: 'Mother became slightly delirious, so now, to calm her down, we are going to open her birthday presents ...'

BARBARA: Where's our present, Cormac?

SANDY: This is something we brought back from our holidays ... here, Barry.

BARRY: No, you give it to her, Sandy ... you picked it.

SANDY: All right, from me and Barry.

ALICE: Lovely (OPENING IT) Well, what can it be?

CORMAC: (FILMING) 'Great excitement now – mother's last birthday here before she goes into a nursing home.'

ALICE: (HEARS HIM) Barbara, do we need all this filming?

BARBARA: All right Cormac, put that down – you're blinding mammy – and get our present – we're next.

CORMAC: Okay, honey – it's in the camera-bag.

BARRY: (TO ALICE) It's just something Sandy got in Majorca ...

SANDY: (HINT) It's something you can either put on your

72

	dinner table or hang on your wall ...
ALICE:	Oh lovely. *(OPENS IT OUT. LOOKS AT IT)* It's a bull.
BARBARA:	Holy Christ!
	(THE PRESENT IS A DECORATIVE PLATE WITH A LARGE BULL, IN A BULL-FIGHT, ON THE SURFACE. ALICE, LOOKING AT THE BACK, SHOWS IT TO US)
BARRY:	No, it's a plate.
ALICE:	That's a lovely present – a bull.
BARRY:	That's a plate.
SANDY:	Do you like it? Honestly now?
ALICE:	Oh yes, Sandy – if the coffee-maker doesn't waken me up every morning, this certainly will.
SANDY:	Oh good.
BARBARA:	*(TAKES THE PLATE. TO BARRY)* Have you no brains at all?
BARRY:	What?
BARBARA:	We're trying to get her to forget bulls and you're giving her one.
BARRY:	That's a plate.
BARBARA:	With a bull on it – had they nothing else in Spain: no castanets, hats, donkeys ...?
BARRY:	Yes they had and they all had shaggin bulls on them!
SANDY:	*(TO BARRY)* What's wrong?
BARRY:	She said we should have got her castanets.
BARBARA:	Where's ours, Cormac – quick.
CORMAC:	Got it here, honey. *(A PARCEL)*
BARBARA:	Before she has time to think. *(TO ALICE)* Now mammy, this is from Cormac and I – Happy birthday. Film it Cormac.
ALICE:	Ah Barbara, you shouldn't have bothered. And Cormac.
CORMAC:	*(FILMS)* Take One – Action!: 'Mother opens the present – looks excited.' *(TURNS TO PICK UP THE PLATE TO FILM IT)* 'Sandy and Barry gave her a ...'
BARBARA:	*(ANGRILY)* Film mammy, Cormac!
CORMAC:	*(BACK TO ALICE)* ' ... a different present. Now to our big moment – will she like it?'
SANDY:	What is it?
ALICE:	Oh, slippers. *(DISAPPOINTED)* Lovely.

BARBARA: To keep your feet warm, mammy ...

BARRY: *(INTO THE CAMERA)* She *has* slippers ...

ALICE: And what's this – a dressing-gown, is it?

BARBARA: Pure wool, mammy – Cormac and I thought slippers and a dressing-gown would be exactly what you'd need when you go to one of those lovely nursing homes – and won't you look lovely meeting all your new friends and wearing these – won't you, mammy? Yes you will. All right, mammy?

ALICE: *(UNENTHUSIASTIC)* Grand.

CORMAC: And we also brought this year's brochures of the nursing homes – we had them sent out – and there are really wonderful improvements everywhere.

BARBARA: And we will tell you all about those after you cut your cake, which we will do now.

BARRY: We still have our present, Barbara.

BARBARA: Oh sorry, Barry – *(TO ALICE)* And after Barry's present, then the cake and then the brochures ...

SANDY: *(TO ALICE)* I'm really sorry about the plate.

ALICE: The plate is lovely ...

SANDY: *(TO ALICE)* If I thought you wanted to play the castanets I would have got you castanets.

ALICE: Pardon?

SANDY: *(TO ALICE)* My granny, who is 90, plays the mouth-organ ...

BARBARA: Sandy, do you mind ...?

SANDY: ... she just takes out her false-teeth and starts sucking and blowing and all the family join in ...

BARBARA: Sandy, can we please get to your present before the whole day goes talking rubbish. *(ANGRILY)* Cormac, are you filming that animal? *(THE PLATE)*

CORMAC: No honey. *(STOPS FILMING IT)*

BARBARA: I'll be checking that film later.
(BARBARA TAKES THE PLATE AND THROWS IT INTO THE RUBBISH BIN. AS)

BARRY: Okay, ma – here it is ...

ALICE: What is it at all?

BARRY: Okay, rip it open, Sandy.

BARBARA: Oh great, I know what it is – it is a commode – well done, Barry, she'll need that.

SANDY: *(TEARING OFF THE PAPER)* No, not a commode ...
BARRY: *(PAPER OFF)* It's a rocking chair!
BARBARA: *(HORRIFIED)* A rocking chair? What good's a rock-
             ing chair?!
ALICE: *(DELIGHTED)* Oh isn't it lovely? I always dreamed
             of having a rocking chair.
BARRY: Well your dream has come true, ma.
CORMAC: *(COMMENTARY)* 'And the gift is a rocking chair'.
BARBARA: Shut up, Cormac.
SANDY: Sit into it. *(ALICE HAPPILY SITS INTO IT)*
BARBARA: *(TO BARRY)* What the hell are you giving her a rock-
             ing chair for?
BARRY: Why not?
BARBARA: They're going to let her smuggle a rocking chair into
             a nursing home, are they?
BARRY: This is before she goes into the home.
BARBARA: But she's going in now – we're picking one today,
             we're phoning today, we're wasting no more time ...
ALICE: *(ROCKING GENTLY)* Oh this is lovely.
BARBARA: ... and you'd better tell her quick.
BARRY: Okay okay. *(TO ALICE)* Ma, it's only for a while, tem-
             porary
ALICE: It's very comfortable.
BARRY: Well don't get too comfortable ...
SANDY: Why not for Heaven's sake – it's hers and she loves it.
BARBARA: Why didn't you get her a commode or towels or a
             radio for her room ...
BARRY: For Christ sake, don't go on about it.
SANDY: *(TO ALICE)* You're like my granny now.
ALICE: Rock me higher.
             (SANDY ROCKS THE CHAIR. ALICE DELIGHTED)
BARBARA: If she mentions that granny once more I'll split her
             open.
ALICE: *(MERRILY)* Higher ... come on, all rock me higher.
BARBARA: Mammy, that's enough – stop that now and try on
             your dressing-gown and your slippers ...
ALICE: *(EXCITEDLY)* And higher ... rock me over the moon,
             Sandy ... over the moon.
             *(AT THIS MOMENT, THE CHAIR BEGINS TO COME
             TO PIECES. SANDY NERVOUSLY STOPS ROCKING*

AS PARTS COME AWAY IN HER HANDS. ALL RUSH
TO CATCH ALICE. THE CHAIR IS COLLAPSING
UNDER HER. ALICE IS LIFTED FROM THE DEBRIS
AND BACK TO HER CHAIR. ALL AS)

BARBARA: *(PANIC)* Jesus Christ, mammy!

ALICE: Help me ... it's disintegrating ...

BARRY: Grab her, grab her ...

SANDY: What happened?

CORMAC: I have her, I have her ...

BARBARA: *(FURIOUS)* Barry, you are a stupid bastard.

BARRY: Do you think I did this deliberately – do you think I asked for a chair that broke?

BARBARA: Are you all right, mammy?

BARRY: Take it easy, ma.

SANDY: What happened to it?

BARBARA: Does this happen to your bloody granny?

SANDY: No, never – she plays her mouth-organ in her chair.

BARBARA: Well I hope next time her chair collapses – and she swallows her bloody mouth-organ.

BARRY: Barbara, will you calm down.

SANDY: But what happened to it?

BARRY: *(HELPING ALICE)* Sandy, will you shut-up – you're like a bloody parrot there.

SANDY: But what happened to it?

BARRY: *(SUDDENLY FURIOUS)* Are you blind as well as thick – it fell to pieces – the chair we got fell to pieces and it fell to pieces because you must have broken it, shoving it into your bloody car.

SANDY: *(FURIOUS)* I did not – don't you start blaming me.

BARRY: Didn't I tell you and stupid Darren that you'd break it ...

SANDY: We didn't break it.

BARRY: They sell them like that, do they?

SANDY: Yes they do, if they're second-hand.

BARBARA: Second-hand?

BARRY: That wasn't second-hand.

SANDY: I told you to get a new one ...

BARRY: It was a bargain, it wasn't second-hand.

SANDY: Don't tell lies, Barry.

BARRY: ... you broke it, you and your thick brother broke it ...

SANDY: It was cheap and second-hand just like you, Barry ...
BARRY: And you're not cheap?
SANDY: I know what I am ...
BARRY: Jesus, don't we all!
BARBARA: For God's sake!
SANDY: ... and at least I'm not a failure like you – a failure at
           work, at buying plates, at buying rocking chairs ...
CORMAC: *(WITH THE CAMERA. SHOUTS)* Get out of shot,
           Barbara ...
BARRY: *(THREATENING)* I'm warning you, Sandy ...
SANDY: ... you're a failure at everything you do, Barry – and I
           mean that in bed as well. *(RUNS INTO THE GAR-
           DEN. PAUSE)*
BARBARA: For the love of God, what is this?
CORMAC: *(OF THE FILM)* Got it all.
BARRY: That chair was perfect until her and her stupid brother
           started shoving it into the car ...
BARBARA: *(FURIOUS)* Well who cares, Barry, who bloody cares
           – just sort it out and try to remember this is mam-
           my's birthday party and we're all supposed to be en-
           joying ourselves. Are you all right, mammy?
ALICE: *(JUMPS WITH FRIGHT)* Grand.
CORMAC: *(MOVES THE CAMERA TO ALICE)* Just want to get
           a reaction shot, mother.
BARBARA: Cormac, if you don't put that camera down, I'll give
           you a reaction shot in the arse.
CORMAC: *(RETREATS RAPIDLY)* Okay honey.
BARBARA: And now, Barry, I'm off to the loo and I'd appreciate
           it if you'd gather up the remains of your collapsible
           rocking-chair ...
BARRY: There's a guarantee on that ...
BARBARA: ... and maybe they'll give you your money back. And
           Cormac ...
CORMAC: I know, I'll see how Sandy is.
BARBARA: Forget Sandy – didn't you say you wanted to film
           around the house ...?
ALICE: *(CONCERNED)* Oh Barbara ...?
CORMAC: I can do that later.
BARBARA: You'll do it now – get it out of the way.
CORMAC: Sure honey.

BARBARA: And mammy, as soon as we get back, we'll make all the nursing home arrangements *before* your cake, then we can relax. And try on your dressing-gown and slippers – they won't fall to pieces.

ALICE: Barbara, don't ...

BARBARA: Don't worry, mammy, we won't be snooping, just filming. Come on, Cormac. *(GOES)*

CORMAC: *(FOLLOWING HER)* Have you got all your pills with you, honey?

(BARBARA AND CORMAC GO. BARRY COLLECTS BITS OF THE CHAIR. THEN)

BARRY: Sorry about the chair, ma.

ALICE: I got the feel of it anyway.

BARRY: And Sandy!

ALICE: You shouldn't fight with her, Barry.

BARRY: Sandy? Sandy loves rowing – she picks rows. Water off a duck with Sandy. Same as her brother Darren and Darlene – all love rows. *(AS HE CLEARS UP, AS MUCH TO HIMSELF NOW)* Not me though – rows effect me, effect sales. But does Sandy understand that? Never. Say what you like about Valerie, but Valerie understood. *(DIRECTLY TO ALICE)* You always liked Valerie, didn't you, ma?

ALICE: *(FROM HER THOUGHTS)* Pardon, Barry?

BARRY: You always got on with Valerie, didn't you?

ALICE: I did – and I wish you did too, Barry.

BARRY: *(LIGHTLY)* I do, who said I don't – we just have our differences – but Val and me are, basically, well, let's face it, we're husband and wife.

ALICE: And the children are growing up very quickly.

BARRY: I know they are, ma. *(THEN)* Reminds me, you wouldn't mind if I ... *(THE PHONE)* ... just to say I've arrived – Val would be glad to know that.

(HE LIFTS THE COSY FROM THE PHONE AND DIALS. THEN)

BARRY: *(INTO PHONE)* Ah Valerie, I've just arrived and I thought I'd ... *(STOPS)* It's me – Barry! *(THEN)* What baby – who told you about any baby? *(SHOUTS)* Don't slam it down, Valerie!

(DURING THIS, ALICE BEGINS TO REMEMBER

*AND WE HEAR THE TINKLING PIANO BEGIN TO
PLAY 'BUBBLES' – THE SKY OUTSIDE DARKENS
AND JIMMY COMES IN. BARRY, ON THE PHONE,
HOLDS THE FREEZE, AS)*

JIMMY: It's been a desperate two months, Alice.

ALICE: But they're going to do nothing?

JIMMY: They're doing nothing because they've nothing to do, Alice.

ALICE: That's what I mean, Jimmy – it's all clear?

JIMMY: Oh a clean slate of the whole thing and they were all apologies once they decided there was no case, that Mona died accidentally from head injuries sustained in her fall from the chair onto the stone floor.

ALICE: Ah that's great news. I mean the Lord have mercy on her soul ...

JIMMY: I know, Alice – I feel the same myself: glad it's all over, but sorry it happened at all. Maybe she was lying there dying, calling out for me ... and I should have fixed that oul chair ...

ALICE: She probably wasn't, Jimmy.

JIMMY: And maybe I drank the milk, maybe I didn't. But it's all over now.

ALICE: And I'm glad, Jimmy.

JIMMY: *(TO ALICE)* But you always believed me, didn't you, Alice? – about Mona and about Walter, even when the police said ...

ALICE: Of course I did, Jimmy.

JIMMY: Thanks Alice. The neighbours didn't and them two nephews of mine didn't – I could see by the looks on their faces. *(STANDS)* I must take them bars off that window for you ...

ALICE: I'm nearly used to them now.

JIMMY: No – it'll give me something to do.

ALICE: Don't be bothering yourself.

JIMMY: *(THEN. NERVOUSLY)* Alice, Mona left me well-off, I have some money and I have my army pension and I have the house and I'm in good health and I'm not getting any younger – do you know what I'm saying, Alice?

ALICE: That your not getting any younger?

JIMMY: *(TO ALICE)* No what I'm saying is, if I had the nerve to say it, though I'm not saying it now, only wondering, but if I had the nerve to say it, do you ever think we could make a fist of it, you and me, together, Alice.

ALICE: What?

JIMMY: *(TO ALICE)* Well don't say Yes or No now but, like, you always did believe me, didn't you, Alice – didn't you?

(JIMMY BEGINS TO RETREAT TOWARDS THE DOOR)

JIMMY: *(AS HE GOES. TO HIMSELF)* You ... always ... did ... believe ... me ...

ALICE: *(DISTRESSED)* Oh Jimmy yes ... and no, Yes and No. And Yes and No, Yes and No and No and Yes *(SHOUTS TO HERSELF)* and Yes and No ...

BARRY: *(TO ALICE)* Pardon, ma.

(SUDDENLY THE KITCHEN DOOR OPENS. BARBARA STRIDES IN, FOLLOWED BY CORMAC WITH HIS CAMERA. BARRY SLAMS DOWN THE PHONE, AND IS SEEN BY BARBARA. THE LIGHT APPEARS OUTSIDE, THE MUSIC STOPS AND JIMMY IS GONE, BY THE BACK DOOR)

BARBARA: Mammy? I want to ask you something.

ALICE: *(SURPRISED FROM HER DREAM)* Yes? What? Oh it's you, Barbara.

BARBARA: Are you on the phone, Barry?

BARRY: *(GUILTILY)* No, just looking at it.

BARBARA: Cormac, film that phone and we'll send it on to Barry – he seems to be obsessed by it.

BARRY: Ah, you took your pills, did you?

BARBARA: You are on thin ice, Barry. Mammy, do you know there is a room locked upstairs?

CORMAC: Filmed everywhere else – couldn't open that door.

ALICE: Oh yes, I know about that.

BARBARA: *(ANNOYED)* There's a reason for that, is there?

ALICE: *(THEN)* Yes.

BARBARA: Yes! Is that the only answer you are going to give me?

ALICE: It has to be, yes.

BARBARA: *(ANNOYED)* Fine, mammy, thank you, great. And

I'm to go home and worry about that too, am I? Like hell I am. Where's the brochures, Cormac? – the messing is over.

(SANDY COMES IN FROM THE GARDEN)

CORMAC: Ah Sandy – you okay?

SANDY: Yes, thank you.

ALICE: Come in, Sandy – and thanks for the chair, even though ...

SANDY: That's all right. *(TO ALL)* And I'm dreadfully sorry if I upset the party again ...

BARBARA: That's okay Sandy – we're now getting on to ...

SANDY: ... but out there I was working out why I get upset every time ...

BARRY: All right, Sandy, why don't we talk it out later?

SANDY: All right, but I worked out that the reason I get upset is ...

BARRY; Later, Sandy!

SANDY: It's just that I only feel threatened by Valerie while I'm in Ireland ...

BARRY: Okay, later, Sandy.

SANDY: ... and I'm sure when we're married in England I won't feel threatened ...

BARRY: Okay ...

SANDY: ... but here every time I hear her name mentioned, I do feel threatened ...

BARRY: *(HARD)* Don't go on, Sandy – I have the message and you won't feel threatened again because her name won't be mentioned again, okay? Over to you, Barbara.

BARBARA: Good. Brochures, Cormac.

CORMAC: Sure honey. *(GIVES BARBARA THE BROCHURES)*

BARBARA: Okay mammy, down to business. To put what we are about to do in context, this day last year I was very disappointed with you, because we had arranged everything and you not only brought in Mr Heffernan ...

BARRY: Mad Heffernan ...

BARBARA: But said that he and his wife ...

BARRY: Mad Mona ...

BARBARA: ... were going to look after you ...

ALICE: Mr Heffernan's wife died.

BARRY: Did she? When?

BARBARA: Cormac and I know that, mammy – we also know how she died ...

BARRY: How do you know that?

CORMAC: From your wife, Valerie.

BARBARA: Valerie gave me all the details ...

SANDY: Now this is why I feel threatened!

BARRY: I'm not mentioning her name – they are. *(TO BARBARA)* I never heard Mad Mona died ...

BARBARA: She died a violent death and when I heard of it, I suffered months of the most awful nightmares, wondering what was going to happen to you, mammy.

ALICE: Me?

BARBARA: Because even though you assured me you weren't seeing him, I still knew he had killed his wife ...

BARRY: Killed her?

BARBARA: Mona Heffernan died from a fractured skull and the police questioned him for days ...

ALICE: Yes but ...

BARBARA: ... because they suspected that he not only murdered her, but he watched her dying with his hearing aid turned off ...

BARRY: What?

CORMAC: And while he was watching ...

BARBARA: I'm telling it, Cormac! And while he was watching her dying, in her own blood, he then proceeded to drink her milk ...

BARRY: Oh Jesus Christ!

BARBARA: ... that was poured out in a glass with two biscuits ...

BARRY: *(RELIEVED)* Oh.

ALICE: No Barbara, the police later said ...

BARBARA: But because the police couldn't prove anything, he was set free – and does that not remind you of the death of our own dear father at the hands of the same man?

BARRY: Jesus Christ!

BARBARA: And that's why, when I heard this out in California ...

CORMAC: Nightmares every night – I got one on video.

BARBARA: ... because I knew he'd strike again and that any day we'd get a phone-call to say mammy had been found butchered ...

CORMAC: I have you saying that on video.

BARBARA: And I also said the only way she'd survive would be for her to kill him first – and could you see that happening?

CORMAC: Against a double murderer who had served time in the army?

BARBARA: So, in context, what we are doing today marks the end to all those nightmares – for you, mammy, as well as for me. Very soon, you will be in a lovely nursing home, with no chance of him coming near you, and we will be able to get on with our lives and begin to make plans again.

SANDY: I think she's going asleep.

BARBARA: (LOUDLY) Mammy, are you listening?

ALICE: (JUMPS) Yes – I was just thinking.

SANDY: My granny does that.

BARBARA: Well, not now, mammy, because now Cormac is going to remind us again of the two lovely nursing homes and when you choose one, we will be making the telephone calls. (HARDER) Okay Cormac, let's go.

CORMAC: Okay honey. Right, mother, what we are talking about here, basically, are the same two as last year: Chestnut Grove and Daffodil Downs, both now enhanced with their own individual improvements ...

SANDY: That's just like CNN.

CORMAC: Thank you, Sandy.

BARBARA: Get on with it, Cormac.

CORMAC: Sure honey. So let me read you from their current brochures – first, Chestnut Grove. (READS) 'Welcome to Chestnut Grove, a home from home for those of us who yearn for peace and tranquillity in our later years; a haven for recollection and recovery for those of us who have been beset by a debilitating illness ...'
(ALREADY THE 'BUBBLES' MUSIC IS HEARD – BUT NOW IT HAS A THREATENING OR SINISTER QUALITY TO IT. A STRANGE LIGHT, NOT SEEN BEFORE, APPEARS, THROWING SHADOWS ON

THE BACK WALL. THE OUTSIDE IS DARKER FOR ALICE'S DISTRESSED THINKING ... AS ALL FREEZE INTO CORMAC'S READING. ALICE MOVES AROUND, AS)

ALICE: Oh Jimmy, how could I ever marry you – I'm too old to be making those kinds of decisions – if only you were here, I could talk to you, but when you're away, I get these nightmares about what would happen ... sometimes when I can't see you, Jimmy, I feel I don't know you at all, I have no idea of what kind of man you really are. Then all they say about you comes into my mind – I don't believe any of it and I know Valerie is only telling me these things for my own good – and merciful God the things she says about Walter and your Mona – why do I even listen to her going on about the newspapers and the books she's read about lonely old women and strange men and murderers and stranglers and the feeling the old woman gets when she thought she was alone in the house but the police knew the murderer was in there too and they tried to telephone her to warn her, but it was too late because the murderer was already in the room, sneaking up behind her and he suddenly heard the telephone and ...

(THE PHONE SUDDENLY RINGS. IT SEEMS VERY LOUD. AS IT RINGS, THE NORMAL LIGHTS CHANGE BACK. THE MUSIC STOPS. ALICE, BACK IN HER CHAIR, CRIES OUT FROM HER DISTRESSED THOUGHTS)

ALICE: *(SHOUTS)* There it is – the police – kill him, kill him first, Barbara says kill him first before he kills me ...

BARBARA: Mammy! Mammy! Stop it, stop shouting! Mammy!

ALICE: *(LOOKS AROUND)* Shouting? Who's shouting?

BARBARA: You were shouting, mammy – what were you shouting for?

BARRY: Was it a dream, ma, or what?

ALICE: *(CONFUSED)* It was, wasn't it? Wasn't it only a dream – amn't I all right?

BARBARA: My God, this is awful – I never knew it was as bad as this – do you often do this, mammy?

SANDY:	The phone's ringing.
BARRY:	Leave it. How do you feel, ma?
ALICE:	I'm grand now, grand. It was a dream.
BARBARA:	Get her a glass of iced water, Cormac.
CORMAC:	Sure honey. *(GOES TO THE SINK)*
BARBARA:	This is not good for me at all – seeing this.
ALICE:	Sorry love, I'm all right now – and the telephone's ringing.
BARBARA:	I'm getting it and this decides everything: it has to be a nursing home and it has to be today. *(INTO THE PHONE)* Hello.
ALICE:	*(LOUDLY)* I don't want a nursing home!
CORMAC:	*(WITH THE WATER)* Drink this slowly, mother.
SANDY:	I think she is tired – my granny often gets tired ...
BARBARA:	*(INTO PHONE)* No, it's great to hear from you, Valerie.
BARRY:	*(QUICKLY)* Barbara, I'm *not* speaking to her
SANDY:	It's her! I don't believe this!
BARRY:	I said I'm *not* speaking to her.
BARBARA:	Of course we'll see you while we're here ...
SANDY:	Are you seeing her, Barry, are you?
BARRY:	What would I be seeing her for – she's talking about her and Cormac – I have nothing to do with her.
BARBARA:	I'll ask him. *(TO BARRY)* Barry, did you slam the phone down on Valerie?
BARRY:	Me? I haven't been speaking to her for over a year – is she drinking again?
BARBARA:	*(INTO PHONE)* He says he didn't, Valerie.
SANDY:	*(ANNOYED)* I don't think I want to stay here much longer.
BARRY:	Relax, Sandy – she's drinking again. *(ARM AROUND HER)*
BARBARA:	*(INTO THE PHONE)* She's okay, but she just had a very frightening attack ...
ALICE:	I didn't, I'm grand.
BARBARA:	So we're arranging a nursing home for her immediately – get her to pack a few things.
ALICE:	*(ANXIOUSLY)* There's nothing wrong with me – will you all just leave me alone.
CORMAC:	It's for your own good, mother.

ALICE: It was only a dream I was having ...
BARBARA: *(INTO PHONE)* Is it? Empty? And where's he?
ALICE: *(A SUDDEN NEW ANXIETY)* Oh Barry, tell Barbara
            to leave the phone, tell her we'll cut the cake now ...
            bring her over.
CORMAC: No mother, we must choose the nursing home first.
BARRY: Then it's the cake ...
BARBARA: *(INTO THE PHONE)* Damn sure I'll ask her.
ALICE: Then get her over to do that.
CORMAC: To choose the nursing home?
ALICE: Yes, you read it out – just don't have her on that phone.
CORMAC: Barbara, she wants to pick the nursing home.
ALICE: *(ANXIOUSLY)* Get her over now!
CORMAC: Barbara, come on quick.
BARRY: She's all set to go, Barbara.
BARBARA: *(INTO PHONE)* Okay Valerie, I'll call you back. *(PUTS
            THE PHONE DOWN)*
CORMAC: Barbara, mother wants me to continue so she can
            select ...
BARBARA: Just hold it, Cormac ...
BARRY: Is Valerie drinking? – she must be drinking if she
            thinks I was talking to her ...
BARBARA: Hold it, Barry! *(CAREFULLY)* Mammy, in that attack
            you had a few minutes ago ...
ALICE: That was a dream, not an attack ...
BARBARA: Whatever it was – you shouted out about killing some-
            one and the police coming ...
ALICE: No I didn't ...
CORMAC: You sure did, mother.
BARBARA: You did and now Valerie tells me that Mr Heffer-
            nan's house is empty, that the grass is overgrown in
            his garden and he hasn't been seen for weeks ...
BARRY: Has he gone away?
CORMAC: Hasn't died, has he?
BARBARA: And there's a room upstairs that is locked and, mam-
            my, you have refused to say why.
CORMAC: Oh Jesus Christ, you don't mean ...?
BARBARA: Mammy, why did you shout out just now about
            killing someone ..?
BARRY: She said, 'murderer, I'll kill the murderer' ...

BARBARA: You said, 'I'll kill him before he kills me'...

SANDY: No, she said ...

BARBARA: Mammy, what's in that locked room? – answer me this minute, mammy.

ALICE: There's nothing in it, nothing.

BARRY: Will I get the cop next door?

BARBARA: *(PANIC)* Mammy, you tell me or we'll find out – what have you hidden in that locked room ...?

ALICE: Nothing ... I don't want any of you to go near that room.

BARBARA: That's it – I'm going to see. Come on Cormac. *(RUNS OUT)*

ALICE: No, Barbara, don't ... please.

CORMAC: Get my camera. *(GRABS HIS CAMERA AND GOES AFTER BARBARA)* Come on, Barry.

BARRY: Sandy, you stay here and watch her. *(RUNS AFTER CORMAC)*

ALICE: Oh God help us now.

SANDY: *(QUIETLY)* My granny sometimes wakes up suddenly and shouts out that she wants to go to a dance – was it like that, just a dream? – was that all it was?

ALICE: Sandy, why don't you meet some nice young fellow?

SANDY: Pardon me?

ALICE: Why don't you meet someone of your own age ...?

SANDY: I see. You don't like me much, do you?

ALICE: I'm telling you this because I do like you.

SANDY: Yes, I've heard that one before.

(A SUDDEN CRASH UPSTAIRS. SOME SHOUTS)

SANDY: *(TO ALICE)* What's that?

ALICE: Ah they'll be down soon now.

(ANOTHER CRASH AND A SCREAM FROM BARBARA)

SANDY: Oh my God. *(STANDS)*

BARRY: *(OFF)* Come on, Barbara – we'll go down.

BARBARA: *(OFF)* Jesus Christ, I can't believe it!

(PAUSE. THEN BARBARA, BARRY AND CORMAC COME SLOWLY IN. SHAKEN)

CORMAC: Got it all on film.

BARBARA: Mammy!

CORMAC: CNN will take this for sure.

BARRY: And you said there was nothing there, ma.

CORMAC: Barry broke down the door ...

ALICE: Ah you didn't break down my good door ...

BARBARA: Never mind the door – mammy, I don't believe this, I do not believe what I've just seen.

BARRY: All the time we were here, that ... *(LOST FOR WORDS)* ... was up there.

ALICE: You found him, did you?

BARBARA: Of course we found him. How could you? – in this house?

SANDY: Oh my God!

ALICE: And what did you do?

BARRY: Well what the hell could we do but look at him.

SANDY: And is he ... (dead)?

CORMAC: Yeah, lying in the bed ...

BARRY: In striped pyjamas ...

BARBARA: With that same smirk on his face and then saying 'Hello there, Barbara, how are you?'

SANDY: He's dead and he spoke?

BARRY: Is that your bed, ma?

ALICE: No.

BARBARA: All the time we've been down here, that murderer was up there, probably listening to everything we said.

SANDY: *(DELIGHTED)* So he's alive?

CORMAC: Yeah – and looking just like Charles Manson.

SANDY: And where is he now?

CORMAC: Manson is in California State Penitentiary.

BARBARA: Cormac, don't be a gobshite all your life! Mammy, how could you do it?

ALICE: I had to do it, Barbara – there was no choice.

BARRY: He forced you?

BARBARA: I knew it! I knew it!

ALICE: No, his nephews wanted to put him into a nursing home – they said he couldn't manage without his wife and he'd have to go whether he liked it or not ...

BARBARA: So ...?

ALICE: So he tried to hide for a while, to go away, staying in digs, no one knew where he was and then ...

BARBARA: And then you locked him up here, in our house?

ALICE: No, Barbara – then I married him.

BARRY: You what?

ALICE: I had my doubts for a while, oh terrible nightmares, but then ...

BARBARA: You're married to ...?! Jesus, a drink, Cormac, quick!

CORMAC: And when did this wedding take place ...?

BARBARA: Get me a drink, Cormac! Mammy, is this a joke?

ALICE: Oh marriage is not a joke, Barbara.

CORMAC: *(GOES TO THE DRINKS)* Valerie never said anything about a wedding, did she?

BARRY: Not a word. *(REALISES. CORRECTS)* Did she Barbara?

BARBARA: No, she did not.

ALICE: We didn't tell Valerie because we wanted a quiet wedding.

BARBARA: And when were you going to tell us – when we were on our way home – when we could do nothing about it? *(TAKES THE DRINK)* Jesus Cormac, did you ever hear anything like this in your life?

CORMAC: Well there was an old Mexican guy I once filmed ...

BARBARA: It's just disgusting – mammy do you know how old you are ...

BARRY: And how old he is ...

BARBARA: ... and he's only out to get this house, everything you own – the way he got daddy's van – and for God's sake what are you both going to do together in this marriage?

BARRY: Jesus, that doesn't bear thinking about.

BARBARA: Well, this is not going to continue – I am going to see that you get a separation or something, mammy – there are grounds for an annulment here ... that man is a degenerate, he's insane ... mammy, he's a serial killer.

(JIMMY APPEARS IN THE DOORWAY. HIS SHIRT IS UNBUTTONED, HAVING PULLED ON HIS CLOTHES)

ALICE: Ah Jimmy.

JIMMY: They broke down the door, Alice.

ALICE: Don't worry about it, Jimmy.

JIMMY: *(OF THE ROCKING CHAIR)* Did they break that

	chair too?
ALICE:	Don't be worrying ... come in and sit down.
BARRY:	Yes, come in and we'll give you a few other things to worry about – or maybe you still can't hear what you don't want to hear.
JIMMY:	Ah hello again, son – no, I have a new hearing aid now.
ALICE:	I gave it to him.
JIMMY:	It fits inside the ear, son, and it's the best yet.
BARRY:	What are you calling me? Ma, why the hell is he calling me that?
JIMMY:	Calling you what?
BARRY:	You know bloody-well what.
BARBARA:	Mammy why is he saying that?
BARRY:	I had this last year and I was worried sick for months ...
ALICE:	Barry, it doesn't mean anything ...
JIMMY:	It's only an expression, son.
BARRY:	It's not an expression – and stop calling me it.
JIMMY:	I call every young fella I meet 'son'.
BARRY:	Well don't call me it – or I'll do something to you that'll take your mind off a few things and maybe knock your new hearing aid out through your other ear.
ALICE:	Barry!
BARRY:	I mean it, ma ... he suddenly thinks he can say what he likes, well I'm not you or his wife or my father ...
BARBARA:	Barry is right, mammy – we are taking no more from him ...
JIMMY:	*(TO SANDY)* Ah hello again, miss.
SANDY:	Hello, Mr Heffernan, how are you?
BARBARA:	Will you shut-up and let us deal with this situation ...
JIMMY:	*(TO SANDY)* Did you have the baby yet?
ALICE:	Not any more Jimmy, she lost that baby.
BARRY:	Jesus Christ, what is this? How does *he* know about it?!
ALICE:	I told him, Barry.
BARRY:	What? Him! Is there anyone who doesn't shaggin know!
JIMMY:	*(TO SANDY)* I'm very sorry to hear that, miss ...

SANDY:	Oh thanks very much – yes, it was terrible and all the time I was carrying it I was hoping ...
BARRY:	Sandy, will you for Christ sake shut-up ...
SANDY:	*(ANGRILY)* No, Barry, I won't shut-up – I'm tired being told to shut-up and it's only natural for a girl to talk about her baby – because I wanted to have that baby ...
BARRY:	I wanted it too ...
SANDY:	No, you did not want it ...
BARRY:	Of course I wanted it ...
BARBARA:	Will you both shut-up and let's ...
SANDY:	*(LOUDLY)* You didn't, Barry, because when I told you about the baby, you hit me ...
BARRY:	Don't you start that.
SANDY:	... and that was the first time you hit me ...
JIMMY:	*(TO BARRY)* You hit her?
BARRY.	*(TO JIMMY)* I never ever laid a finger on her ...
SANDY:	You did hit me and then you hit me again and that's how I lost the baby and I wanted it and I thought you wanted it too ...
BARRY:	I did want the shaggin thing ...!
JIMMY:	*(TO SANDY)* Ah you're better off without him, miss.
BARRY:	*(TO JIMMY)* You shut-up or I'll ...
JIMMY:	*(TO BARRY)* No, you shut-up because we know your wife, Valerie ...
BARBARA:	Will you all shut-up and let's talk about mammy ...
JIMMY:	... and your Valerie told Alice that you wrote to her about coming back to Ireland ...
SANDY:	You what?!
BARRY:	That's a damn lie!
JIMMY:	No, Valerie said you said you miss your children ...
SANDY:	Your children?!
BARRY:	*(TO JIMMY)* I'm warning you – one more word ...
JIMMY:	... and still you're leading that young-one up the garden path ...
BARRY:	That's it – you've had it ...
ALICE:	Barry!
	(BARRY RUNS AT JIMMY TO THROW A PUNCH. JIMMY MOVES ASIDE AND EXPERTLY HOLDS BARRY'S ARM AND TWISTS. BARRY FALLS TO

*THE GROUND, AS JIMMY HOLDS HIM. CORMAC
IMMEDIATELY BEGINS TO FILM)*

BARBARA: For God's sake stop!

BARRY: My arm, my bloody arm.

JIMMY: *(ANGRILY TO BARRY)* You're no bloody good are you? – and although I always wanted a son, I would not have you if you were the last young-fella left on earth ...

BARRY: You'll break my bloody arm ...

BARBARA: *(OF HIM FILMING)* Cormac!

JIMMY: Now do the gentlemanly thing and let that young-one go ...

BARRY: All right! Let go my arm ...
(JIMMY RELEASES HIS ARM)

BARRY: You bastard! That proves it – proves what you did to my da, to your wife ...

JIMMY: Sorry Alice, I had to ...

ALICE: That's all right, Jimmy.

BARBARA: Excuse me, mammy, is this how you see your married life – with your husband breaking people's arms on the kitchen floor?

BARRY: That guy is a lunatic, ma.

SANDY: Barry ...?

BARRY: Jesus, yes, what? – what do you want now?

SANDY: I think, Barry, I want to go home.

BARRY: Ah for God's sake ...

SANDY: I mean it, Barry – and I'll take the car, *my* car, and I'll get the ferry tonight ...

BARRY: But you've only arrived ...

SANDY: And you can spend all the time you like with Valerie and the children that you *do* want ...

BARRY: I'm not seeing Valerie or any children ...

SANDY: *(HARD)* The car-keys, Barry.

BARRY: Right, go on, go to hell. *(GIVES HER THE KEYS)*

SANDY: *(SADLY)* Goodbye everybody ... Alice. *(NOW GOES TO ALICE)*

ALICE: *(HOLDS SANDY)* You take my advice now ...

SANDY: I will. Thanks. *(TURNS TO GO)*

BARRY: Sandy, listen – I'll fly back in about a week and we can have a good chat ...

SANDY: *(ANGRILY)* You fly back and you'll be chatting with my brother Darren – and he *will* break your bloody arm! *(GOES)*

BARBARA: *(BARELY CONTROLLED)* Okay mammy, I will say this as calmly as I can: there seems to be little purpose in pursuing this birthday party here or at the restaurant ...

ALICE: Or Jimmy could take Sandy's place in the restaurant ...

BARBARA: ... So what I suggest is we postpone it for a few days ...

BARRY: Ma, you don't mind if I ... *(PICKS UP THE PHONE AND DIALS)*

BARBARA: *(CONTINUING)* ... we postpone it for a few days, due to my jet-lag and to your family crises, while we rest at the Royal Hotel and try to calmly visit some of our friends ...

ALICE: Or you could stay with Jimmy and me ...

CORMAC: Get this on film. *(FILMS)*

BARBARA: *(CONTINUING)* ... and when we have rested I will arrange for all of us to meet again to come to some firm and final decision about (a) your annulment and (b) your nursing home. All right, mammy?

BARRY: *(ANGRILY, OF THE PHONE)* Come on, answer!

ALICE: Grand, Barbara.

BARBARA: Good. And Cormac, switch that thing off before I smash it to pieces.

CORMAC: *(STILL FILMING)* Smash our livelihood to pieces, honey?

BARBARA: *(INTO THE LENS)* If we were depending on that for our livelihood, Cormac, we'd be living on the city dump, and you know it. *(DISCONNECTS HIS LEADS)* Now switch it off and come on! *(GOES)*

CORMAC: Sure honey. *(TO HIMSELF)* I'll wipe that.

BARRY: *(SMASHES THE PHONE DOWN)* Shit! Hey Cormac – could you give me a lift to Valerie's, it's on your way.

CORMAC: Well, Barbara is in a hurry and ...

BARRY: She won't mind.

CORMAC: Okay, let's go. *(GOES)*

BARRY: Bye ma *(KISSES HER)* I'll phone you to arrange whatever ... you're arranging.

ALICE: Goodbye Barry – don't go back without calling over.

BARRY: Right, ma. *(TO JIMMY)* And I haven't finished with you and don't think I have. *(GOES)*

(JIMMY STANDS WITH ALICE)

JIMMY: That was a bad mistake – losing my rag with him.

ALICE: How did you do that – that twisty thing?

JIMMY: I thought I'd forgotten how – but the way he was treating that poor young one ...

ALICE: You were right to do it – if Barry had that earlier in life from Walter or any man, he might've turned out better.

JIMMY: Aye. *(THEN)* Well, one thing anyway, they know about us now, don't they?

ALICE: Oh they do.

JIMMY: So what do you think?

ALICE: Well, now that they are beginning to get used to the idea, I think we should go ahead, make the arrangements ... and get married.

JIMMY: Only if you're sure and certain, Alice – and sure it's not just to keep the pair of us out of nursing homes.

ALICE: Yes, I'm sure and certain.

JIMMY: I'll be a good husband, Alice.

ALICE: I know you will, Jimmy Heffernan.

JIMMY: Oh jingos, I nearly forgot all about your birthday present.

ALICE: Ah you shouldn't have bothered ...

JIMMY: *(TAKES A SMALL PARCEL FROM THE PRESS)* I only had barely time to hide this and run upstairs before they arrived.

ALICE: Yes and you left the hall-door open and had me blamed.

JIMMY: Well, happy birthday dear Alice. *(GIVES IT TO HER)* *(ALICE OPENS IT. IT IS A BUBBLE JAR AND A BLOWER)*

ALICE: *(DELIGHTED)* Ah, bubbles – from the bubble-boy.

JIMMY: There's an interesting scientific fact about how the air inside a bubble ...

ALICE: *(GENTLY)* Jimmy, maybe I'll just blow one and we can see the scientific fact for ourselves.

JIMMY:	*(GENTLY)* Fair enough.
ALICE:	*(BLOWS SOME BUBBLES. SINGS)* I'm forever blowing bubbles ...
JIMMY:	*(SINGS)* ... pretty bubbles in the air ...
ALICE:	*(SINGS)* ... they fly so high ...
JIMMY:	*(SINGS)* ... they nearly reach the sky ...
ALICE:	(SINGS) ... then like my dreams they fade and die.
JIMMY:	*(TO HER)* Not always, Alice, not always.

(THE SONG IS TAKEN UP ON THE RECORD AS ALICE AND JIMMY EMBRACE

LIGHTS SLOWLY FADE TO DARKNESS – A LONGER LIGHT ON THE PICTURE OF 'BUBBLES' BY MILLAIS, THEN SEEN IN THE DARKNESS. THEN THIS TOO FADES AS THE MUSIC CONTINUES)

THE END

STELLA BY STARLIGHT

This play was first produced at The Gate Theatre Dublin, for the Dublin Theatre Festival, on 8 October 1996, with the following cast:

DERMOT	Tom Hickey
STELLA	Marion O'Dwyer
TARA	Janet Moran
GERALDINE	Gemma Craven
PAUL	Stephen Brennan
TOMMY	Eanna MacLiam

DIRECTOR	Ben Barnes
DESIGNER	Frank Hallinan Flood
LIGHTING	Robert Bryan

FOR GLORIA

*THE LOUNGE OF A CONVERTED, MODERNISED FARM-
HOUSE.*

*AT THE BACK, A BUILT-ON CONSERVATORY: GLASS WIN-
DOWS AND ROOF. A DOOR AT ITS STAGE-RIGHT TO OUT-
SIDE. IN THE ROOF, AN 'AUTOMATIC' SLIDE-ACROSS SEC-
TION. THIS IS NOW OPEN.*

*IN THE LOUNGE, A DOOR TO THE KITCHEN AT STAGE
RIGHT. AT LEFT, A STAIRCASE STARTS IN THE LOUNGE AND
DISAPPEARS OFF TO SECOND-FLOOR BEDROOMS, ETC. (WE
SEE ONLY FIVE/SIX STEPS) A SLIDING-DOOR (TO EXCLUDE
DRAUGHTS) ON THE STAIRS BECOMES PART OF STAGE-LEFT
WALL. THE ENTRANCE DOOR IS UPSTAGE LEFT – THROUGH
A SMALL HALL-WAY WITH A HEAD-HIGH WINDOW, ALLOW-
ING ONE TO SEE INTO THE LOUNGE BEFORE ENTERING.*

*USUAL FURNITURE IN THE LOUNGE. CENTRAL HEAT-
ING RADIATORS. WOODEN FLOOR WITH SCATTER RUGS.
SHELVES WITH BOOKS AND DIY ENCYCLOPAEDIA. AT ONE
RADIATOR, SOME PLUMBING TOOLS. ELSEWHERE, AND
NOTICEABLE, A SHOT-GUN. AT STAGE LEFT, AN ELABORATE
AND DELICATELY WIRED TROPHY OF THE PLANETS HAS
SOME PROMINENCE.*

*IN THE CONSERVATORY, AN OLD DESK WITH A COM-
PUTER, MODEM, FAX AND PHONE. (IDEALLY, WE SHOULD
SEE THE COMPUTER SCREEN WITH ITS CHANGING IMAGES
BUT, IF NOT POSSIBLE IN PRODUCTION, THE SCREEN MAY
BE TURNED AWAY FROM US.) HERE, ALSO, AN OLD SWIVEL
CHAIR ON CASTORS. ALSO A LARGE (6.25 INCH) TELESCOPE
WITH A CAMERA MOUNTED ON IT, CONNECTED BY CABLE
TO THE COMPUTER. NEARBY, A SMALLER TELESCOPE. BOTH
POINT TO THE SKY. STAR CHARTS ON WALLS. A PACKET OF
MARIETTA BISCUITS ON DESK.*

*THE HOUSE IS WELL BEYOND DUBLIN'S OUTER SUB-
URBS, IN THE WICKLOW HILLS. ISOLATED, BUT WITH
'CHARACTER'.*

*IT IS A COLD OCTOBER EVENING, ABOUT EIGHT
O'CLOCK.*

WE OPEN IN DARKNESS. THE MUSIC IS MAJESTIC. A

SPOT PICKS OUT THE TROPHY. ESTABLISH. NOW SPOT FADES, MUSIC FADES, LIGHTS UP. SOUND OF AN INCOMING FAX IS HEARD. WE SEE DERMOT AT THE LARGE TELESCOPE, OBSERVING THE NIGHT SKY. HE IS 50. HE NOW WEARS A BOILER SUIT.

DERMOT: *(LOOKING)* Jupiter, Jupiter, you beautiful lady. *(NOW MOVES AWAY. GOES TO A WALL SWITCH. ANNOUNCES)* Close Observation Window. *(THROWS THE SWITCH. THE CONSERVATORY ROOF-WINDOW CLOSES.*

DERMOT WILL CONTENTEDLY GO TO HIS DESK, SIT INTO HIS SWIVEL CHAIR, KEY-IN VARIOUS INFORMATION ON HIS COMPUTER. THE FAX HAS STOPPED. DERMOT SLIDES OVER IN HIS CHAIR TO RETRIEVE IT AS STELLA OPENS THE SLIDE-DOOR ON THE STAIRS AND ENTERS.

SHE IS 43, SENSIBLY AND WARMLY DRESSED, WEARS GLASSES, IS SLIGHTLY OVER-WEIGHT. SHE CARRIES A DUSTER, FURNITURE SPRAY AND A PORTRAIT-SIZED PHOTO)

STELLA: *(OF THE PHOTO)* Dermot, I was thinking of putting this up somewhere.

DERMOT: *(OF THE FAX)* Listen to this, Stella – from Erik in Stockholm. *(READS)* 'Good luck to you for photographing Jupiter this night. We am all awaiting, with great pregnancy, to seeing your astonishing results. Happy regards – Erik. P.S.: Looking frontways to meeting you someday.'

STELLA: *(AMUSED)* He means well.

DERMOT: *(WARMLY)* 'Looking front-ways'. Deed he does mean well. And nine other faxes in and more on the e-mail – and only seven hours to go. This will be some night, eh Stella? – our finest hour.

STELLA: *(FEELING THE RADIATOR)* Dermot, did you not fix the radiators yet – they're still like ice.

DERMOT: Did you turn on the valve upstairs?

STELLA: Yes, clockwise, like you told me, an hour ago.

DERMOT: *(PRE-OCCUPIED)* Then it's probably an air-lock – I'll look at it in a minute.

STELLA:	You said that two hours ago and it's freezing in here and it'd be terrible if it was still like this when Paul and Geraldine arrive.
DERMOT:	It won't be, Stella – I'll fix it in a minute. *(PROUDLY)* Now, how's it all looking so far?
STELLA:	It looks great. Is that packet of Marietta biscuits supposed to be there?
DERMOT:	What? Oh no no – you can take those out.
STELLA:	And I'll put these books away ...
DERMOT:	Eh no, you can leave them. *(PLACES ONE CARE-FULLY ON THE CHAIR. THEN, OF THE PHOTO-GRAPH)* What's this?
STELLA:	Oh I thought it'd be nice to put that up somewhere before they arrive – do you remember it: the four of us at our Bank's Dinner Dance.
DERMOT:	*(NOT ENTHUSIASTIC)* I didn't know you had that.
STELLA:	I only found it today. *(AMUSED)* Isn't it good? Look at the size of me – and you with hair ... and Paul – I think he was drunk that night.
DERMOT:	And every other night.
STELLA:	And wasn't Geraldine lovely? And remember that was the night the band kept playing for me *(SINGS)* 'That's Stella By Starlight, and not a dream.' I'll put it here.
DERMOT:	Whatever you like, but personally I think it looks a bit peculiar.
STELLA:	Oh no, it'll be nice with Tara going off to her Debs – and remember, it was just after that we started going out together.
DERMOT:	*After* it, yes. But *at* it, as you can see by the way he's hanging out of you, you were with Paul and I was stuck with Geraldine. Now I presume they don't want to be reminded of that night – and I don't think we do either.
STELLA:	*(DISAPPOINTED)* No – you're right. I'll put it away. *(TAKES IT INTO THE KITCHEN)*
DERMOT:	Let's keep the evening simple, I say: Jupiter, Tara off to her Debs, a few drinks, few sandwiches, bit of chat and a good night's sleep.
	(DERMOT NOW CHECKING THE RADIATORS)

STELLA:	*(EMERGES WITH A CARPET-SWEEPER)* Oh, about drinks, Dermot ...
DERMOT:	How's your migraine by the way?
STELLA:	Oh nearly gone completely.
DERMOT:	Good. I'd go easy on the vodka tonight.
STELLA:	Yes. I'll probably only have a sherry or two ...
DERMOT:	*(CONTINUING)* It's the vodka that causes those headaches, not your contact lenses – oh and give yourself time to put those in. And I'm serious about those glasses – they really do put years on you.
STELLA:	It's just that the contact lenses hurt my eyes ...
DERMOT:	Only because you never gave them a chance.
STELLA:	I suppose so. But about the drinks, Dermot, you will remember that the mineral water is for Paul ...
DERMOT:	*(MERRILY)* So Paul the playboy now drinks mineral water!
STELLA:	No, seriously, Dermot, Geraldine specifically said ...
DERMOT:	I know, I know, he's in training to play golf with the Japanese ...
STELLA:	She said it's an important business crowd that's coming over ...
DERMOT:	... and he's afraid of getting the shakes – don't worry, he won't be tempted tonight – he can drink whatever he likes as far as I'm concerned.
STELLA:	It wouldn't be fair. *(THEN. OF THE RADIATOR)* Is it getting hot at all?
DERMOT:	Will you give me a chance, Stella! I first have to make certain that there *is* an air-lock, otherwise when I turn this key to release the trapped air, I'm likely to get a jet of water into my face ... Oh Christ! *(DERMOT HAS TURNED THE KEY. A JET OF WATER SPURTS OUT AT HIM. HE TURNS IT OFF, AS)*
DERMOT:	Stella, how often do I have to say it?: stop looking at me while I'm trying to do things.
STELLA:	Sorry Dermot.
DERMOT:	Okay, now we know that it's not an air-lock, so now all we have to do is go down through our check-list to see what the problem really is. *(OPENS A DIY ENCYCLOPAEDIA)* But no panic, nothing to worry

	about, as long as you have the books and the know-how. *(TURNING PAGES)* H ... H ... H ... hacksaws, hammers, hammocks, harps, hatchets, here we are – heating ... now, heating problems.
TARA:	*(FROM UPSTAIRS. ANGRILY)* Oh for God's sake! *(CALLS)* Mum!
STELLA:	*(CALLS)* Tara, don't turn on the water yet.
DERMOT:	Can she not wait five minutes! I told her not to touch that water until I'd fixed it.
STELLA:	Dermot, she has to shower – it's gone eight and Sean could be here any minute.
DERMOT:	Who?
STELLA:	The fellow who's taking her to the Debs – the engineer.
DERMOT:	His name isn't Sean, it's Tom.
STELLA:	*(URGENTLY)* No, it's Sean Connery – I remembered it because it's the same as the film star.
DERMOT:	I know – that's how I know it's Tom Cruise.
STELLA:	No ...
DERMOT:	Yes – it's Tom Cruise.
STELLA:	No – Sean Connery.
DERMOT:	Tom Cruise!
	(TARA (17) COMES DOWN THE STAIRS. BARE FEET, JEANS AND A SWEATER)
TARA:	*(ANGRY AND UPSET)* Dad, what's wrong? the water is still freezing!
DERMOT:	Tara, if you'd just wait until I ...
TARA:	Daddy, I've been waiting a whole hour while you were messing with your telescopes.
DERMOT:	I was not messing – tonight happens to be the most important astronomical night since ...
TARA:	And it also happens to be my Debs ...
STELLA:	Tara!
TARA:	... and an hour ago, I was promised a bath, then it was a shower and now there's still no hot water and any minute there's going to be a ring at that door and ...
DERMOT:	Five minutes, Tara, give me five minutes and you'll have enough time to have ten showers before Tom Cruise ever gets here.

STELLA:	Sean Connery!
TARA:	*(FURIOUS)* For God's sake, his name is Tony Curtis!
DERMOT:	Tony Curtis! Since when?
TARA:	Since always – and I'm sorry I'm going to this bloody Debs with him or with anyone and I hate this freezing house and I don't know what was wrong with Terenure or why we had to move out of it up to the bloody Himalayas.
DERMOT:	*(CONTROLLED)* This is not the Himalayas – it is the beautiful Wicklow Hills where everybody would love to live if you gave them the chance.
TARA:	Yes, if they happened to be the Von Trapp Family.
STELLA:	Tara!
DERMOT:	No Tara, if they happened to appreciate good, healthy, safe living and your mother and I made great sacrifices for this and the least we expect is a bit of gratitude, especially tonight when we have visitors.
TARA:	Oh at last, visitors!
DERMOT:	*(WITH HIS TOOL-BOX)* Stella, when you turned the valve, was it the left one or the right one?
STELLA:	You said anti-clockwise ...
DERMOT:	But was it the hot or the cold, on the left or on the right?
STELLA:	I'm not sure. I'll go and see ...
DERMOT:	Leave it, leave it, I'll go.
STELLA:	*(ON THE STAIRS)* No, I can ...
DERMOT:	I said I'll go – you come down, feel the rad and tell me if it gets hot. And don't anyone touch the telescope – and Tara, this is not messing – photographing the first comet crash on Jupiter for over a hundred years, does not constitute messing! *(STELLA HAS RETURNED. DERMOT GOES, CLOSING THE SLIDING DOOR)*
TARA:	This is all your fault, mum.
STELLA:	I beg your pardon?
TARA:	You should never have asked them over – that's what has him going around like that ... making the big impression ... showing off his DIY – look at that

shelf, bang and hang *(TOUCHES IT. IT SLIPS)* ... it's a joke ... and the floor's a death-trap ... and planting these weird books all over the house *(PICKS UP THE BOOK THAT DERMOT PLACED EARLIER) The Politics of Greed and Alienation in the Age of Deconstruction!* It's pathetic. *(THROWS IT ASIDE)*

STELLA: *(REPLACES THE BOOK)* As a matter of fact, I put that there, so leave it and don't touch anything else – *(RESETS THE SLIPPED SHELF)* – and they are invited because we haven't seen them for years, because Geraldine is my friend ...

TARA: But Paul! You know daddy hates his guts ever since he was kept on and Daddy was let go.

STELLA. *(STOPS. CHECKS THE SLIDING DOOR IS CLOSED. GOES ANGRILY TO TARA)* Tara, your father was never let go – he took Early Retirement.

TARA: Get real, mum – he was booted out.

STELLA: He was not and don't you ever say that again. And, anyway, he's been looking forward to Paul coming all week.

TARA: Only so he can shove all this in his face.

STELLA: No, so they can both see you going off and ...

TARA: Me? For God's sake, I'm only going to a dance.

STELLA: *(CROSSLY)* Tara, they are your god-parents and if they had children of their own they mightn't be so concerned but as they haven't they are.

TARA: *(LOST)* What?

STELLA: So you be nice to them – this evening, tonight and tomorrow.

TARA: *(CALMER)* You think I never went out with a fellow before. *(STELLA LOOKS AT HER)* All right, I didn't! – but that's no reason for all this messing: embarrassing me, embarrassing Tony – as if he wasn't embarrassed enough when I had to ask him to go with me.

STELLA: *(GENTLY)* I'm sure he was delighted.

TARA: Oh he was – once I said I was buying the tickets. But you should have heard him when I told him where I lived.

STELLA: Now Tara ...

TARA:	And he was right: asking me did we milk our own cows and when we order a piazza does it take a week to get here, and do we get snowed-in in the winter – and Mum, am I the only one who thinks it's like the Artic in here? *(DERMOT COMES ANGRILY DOWN THE STAIRS)*
DERMOT:	Stella, I thought you were feeling the radiator for me!
STELLA:	Oh sorry, Dermot, I was just going to ...
DERMOT:	*(AHEAD OF HER)* Leave it, I'll do it.
STELLA:	No, I can ...
DERMOT:	I said leave it. *(FEELS IT. COLD)* If only I was left to do these things the way I want to. *(OF HIS COM-PUTER)* Is that a fax I see coming in?
STELLA:	I'll see where it's from ...
DERMOT:	*(AHEAD OF HER)* I'll get it, I'll get it ... *(THE PHONE RINGS)*
DERMOT:	Ah who the hell is that at this hour?
STELLA:	*(GOING)* I'll get it.
DERMOT:	*(AHEAD OF HER)* Leave it, Stella, leave it – I have it. *(DERMOT PICKS UP THE PHONE, AS)*
STELLA:	*(SUDDENLY FURIOUS)* Oh for Christ sake, Dermot, let me do something – I'm not totally useless, you know – I am capable of answering a phone or feeling a bloody radiator! *(DERMOT STOPS)*
DERMOT:	*(INTO THE PHONE)* Just hold a moment, please. *(TO STELLA)* Stella, are you all right?
STELLA:	*(IMMEDIATELY REPENTANT)* Yes, Dermot. Sorry. I'm sorry. *(TAKES OFF HER GLASSES)*
TARA:	Dad, that might be Tony.
DERMOT:	That migraine isn't back, is it?
STELLA:	No, I'm grand. I'm sorry.
DERMOT:	You haven't been at the vodka, have you?
STELLA:	No no.
DERMOT:	It's not Paul coming here, is it?
STELLA:	No, of course not.
DERMOT:	Because if he tries any of his playboy-tactics, he'll

	be out that door, Jupiter or no Jupiter.
STELLA:	It's not that, Dermot.
DERMOT:	Then we've nothing to worry about, Stella.
TARA:	*(ANXIOUSLY)* Dad, that might be Tony!
DERMOT:	*(STERNLY)* Tara, please! *(POLITELY INTO PHONE)* Just hold a moment please. *(GENTLY TO STELLA)* Stella, tonight is a celebration: our new house, all we've done here, Tara going to her Debs, Jupiter ...
STELLA:	I know, Dermot – it's just that ...
DERMOT:	... and don't worry about the heat, I'll have that going before anyone gets here.
STELLA:	I know, Dermot – it's just that ...
DERMOT:	And you have no idea how well you look without those glasses. Honestly now.
TARA:	*(OF THE PHONE)* Please Dad ...
STELLA:	Thank you, Dermot – it's just that I can do things if you let me. That's all.
DERMOT:	Of course you can, Stella – who said you can't. And everything else is firmly under control. Okay?
STELLA:	Yes Dermot.
DERMOT:	Excellent. And I'd put in your contact lenses, soon as you can.
TARA:	*(ANGRILY)* Dad, if you're not going to talk on that phone ...
DERMOT:	Tara! *(INTO THE PHONE)* Hello – apologies for that ... *(THEN)* Geraldine! *(HAPPILY TO STELLA)* It's Geraldine! *(INTO THE PHONE)* Have you not left your house yet? The comet is on its way, you know.
TARA:	*(TO STELLA)* Is it hot, mum – can I have my shower now?
STELLA:	*(FEELING THE RADIATOR)* Maybe at the bottom.
DERMOT:	*(INTO THE PHONE)* Oh, a car phone? So where are you?
TARA:	*(AT THE RADIATOR)* Good God, it's still freezing!
STELLA:	No, the bottom is hot.
TARA:	Meaning what? – that I can now wash my feet? *(ANGRILY)* Dad!
DERMOT:	*(INTO THE PHONE)* Then you're only five minutes from us. *(TO STELLA. SUDDEN PANIC)* They're

nearly here and look at me! *(INTO THE PHONE)* Grand. Go over that bridge and straight for two miles ...

TARA: Dad, the water is still freezing ...

STELLA: Dermot, I'm going to put in my contact lenses. *(GOING UPSTAIRS)*

DERMOT: *(INTO THE PHONE)* We're the only house, you can't miss us. *(TO STELLA)* Stella, wait! *(INTO PHONE)* No, Tara is still here – but listen, you might meet Stella – she's out for a walk in the night air.

STELLA: *(STOPS)* What?

DERMOT: *(INTO PHONE)* Oh yes – she went about half an hour ago.

STELLA: I didn't! – I'm putting in my contact lenses.

DERMOT: *(INTO PHONE)* Exactly – just don't run her down. Right, see you in about five minutes. Bye Geraldine. *(DERMOT RINGS OFF AND BEGINS TO ANXIOUSLY PULL OFF HIS DUNGAREES. HE HAS A SHIRT AND TROUSERS UNDER)*

DERMOT: That stupid wagon and her husband are early and look at me.

STELLA: Dermot, I have to put in my contact lenses ...

TARA: Daddy, the water is still freezing ...

DERMOT: *(LOUDLY)* That Astronomy Menu should be up on the screen. *(AS HE DOES THIS)* And Stella, you heard what I said, so you better get your coat on and go. *(TARA RUNS UP TO THE BATHROOM TO CHECK THE WATER, AS)*

STELLA: And go where?

DERMOT: Out in the night air.

STELLA: But for what?

DERMOT: Because I told them that's where you were.

STELLA: But why did you have to do that?

DERMOT: Because the plan is now changed. How can I be out in the night air – I was talking to them.

STELLA: What plan? Why has anyone got to be out in the night air?

DERMOT: *(ANGRILY)* Think, Stella – the whole point of us

108

	living up here is that we live healthily, we go for walks. Their first impression can't be of us all sitting here like rats in a hole.
STELLA:	Then we'll say I was out and I've come back.
DERMOT:	No, you're still out, Stella – I told them – so please get your coat and go.
STELLA:	*(PETULANTLY)* Then I'll have to wear my glasses.
DERMOT:	*(TAKES HER GLASSES)* No, you will not, Stella – put in your contact lenses, put them in now ... *(PUTS HER GLASSES INTO HIS POCKET)*
STELLA:	But they're up in the bathroom ...
TARA:	*(COMES ANGRILY DOWN THE STAIRS)* Daddy, the water is still freezing ...
DERMOT:	Tara, give it a chance – it's on its way.
TARA:	But I have to have it now! *(PANIC)* Mum!
STELLA:	*(STOPS)* Dermot, she has to shower.
DERMOT:	And I have to wash and shave.
STELLA:	But the house is still freezing and Tara has to ...
DERMOT:	Stella, what do you want? It's on its way – I can do no more! I have to get ready and I have to do it now.
TARA:	And what about me?
DERMOT:	Tara, I've no time to argue. *(TO STELLA)* Best if you go out through the kitchen and back in through the conservatory – and, Stella, don't leave me here with them for long; he's an awful gobshite to try and talk to. And take those Marietta biscuits out of here. *(DERMOT GOES QUICKLY UPSTAIRS)*
STELLA:	And when do I put in my contact lenses?
DERMOT:	*(OFF)* Do it now.
STELLA:	*(ANGRILY)* Oh for God's sake!
TARA:	Mum, what do I do about my shower?
STELLA:	For a start, you can stop shouting! As soon as I get back, we'll put on a few saucepans of water, we'll fill the big enamel bucket, and we'll boil them up and you can pour them into the bath with whatever hot water there is. Okay?
TARA:	What?!
STELLA:	*(FURIOUSLY)* Tara, do you have any better ideas?
TARA:	Oh this is great – all my friends are soaking in bubble baths while I'm up the mountains throwing buck-

	ets of water over myself.
STELLA:	*(FEELS AROUND BLINDLY)* Did you see my glasses?
TARA:	And what do I dry myself with? – lumps of grass?
STELLA:	Tara, did you see my glasses anywhere?
	(THE DISTANT SOUND OF A BARKING DOG – AND THEN A SWEEP OF CAR-LIGHTS ACROSS THE CONSERVATORY)
TARA:	Dad put them in his pocket.
STELLA:	What? *(CALLS)* Dermot did you put ...? *(REALISES)* Oh my God, here's Paul and Geraldine. I'll have to go – you let them in.
TARA:	Me?
STELLA:	Say your father is taking a nap.
TARA:	A nap? He's just been talking to them.
STELLA:	Reading a book then – and I'm out taking the night air.
TARA:	And supposing Tony ...?
STELLA:	And I'll put on the water before I go.
	(THE DOOR-BELL RINGS, AS STELLA GOES QUICKLY – AND BLINDLY – OUT THROUGH THE KITCHEN)
TARA:	*(DESPERATELY)* Mum, you shouldn't let dad to this to us!
	(DERMOT APPEARS ON THE STAIRS. HIS SHIRT IS OUTSIDE HIS TROUSERS, SHAVING CREAM ON HIS FACE)
DERMOT:	Tara, is your mother gone yet ...?
TARA:	Yes! She's gone out through the back ...
DERMOT:	Quick, give me those Marietta biscuits – and will you answer that door!
TARA:	*(ANGRILY GIVES HIM THE BISCUITS)* Dad, I have to get ready!
	(DERMOT RUNS BACK UPSTAIRS, CLOSING THE SLIDING DOOR. TARA GOES OUT TO THE HALL DOOR. THE FOLLOWING IS HEARD FROM THE HALL)
TARA:	*(OFF)* Hello – come in, come in.
GERALDINE:	*(OFF)* Tara! Haven't you grown up.
PAUL:	*(OFF)* Hello Tara, shouldn't you be ready?

110

TARA: *(OFF)* Oh it won't take me long ...

GERALDINE: *(OFF)* Oh isn't this lovely – I'm just dying to see this house.

(TARA COMES IN – CHECKING THAT EVERY-ONE IS GONE)

GERALDINE: *(OFF)* Oh Paul, isn't this a wonderful idea? – this little hole in the wall. *(THE WINDOW)*

(GERALDINE AND PAUL ENTER THE ROOM)

TARA: That window was part of the old house – but my dad did all this bit.

GERALDINE: Oh my God – it's wonderful. Paul, isn't this room wonderful?

PAUL: *(UNIMPRESSED)* Wonderful is not the word.

GERALDINE: *(AWARE)* Yes it is, darling. *(TO TARA)* And did your dad build-on that conservatory?

(GERALDINE IS 40, SLIM, VERY ATTRACTIVE IN A GLAMOROUS DRESS BENEATH HER COAT. PAUL IS A TRENDY 48, IN A SUIT. HE HAS AN EXPENSIVE CAMERA AROUND HIS NECK. GER-ALDINE CARRIES CHOCOLATES AND ALSO AN ORCHID IN A GIFT-WRAPPED BOX. BOTH VERY LIVELY)

TARA: Oh yes – he actually re-designed the whole house ... put in new doors, floors, everything.

GERALDINE: And that lovely door up there *(THE SLIDING-DOOR ON THE STAIRCASE)*

TARA: That's to keep out the draughts.

GERALDINE: *(COLD. UNBELIEVING)* Oh is it?

TARA: And he put up all the shelves – and that's his astro-nomy room.

GERALDINE: Isn't he marvellous – Paul, isn't this a marvel?

PAUL: Absolutely. And I see he's on the Internet.

TARA: Oh yes, with all the other astronomers, morning noon and night.

PAUL: That's what the Internet does – takes over your life. *(FEELING THE COLD)* Not chilly, are you, darling?

GERALDINE: Oh no no no – I think we just had the car too warm. *(TO TARA)* Don't start him off on our new car.

PAUL: Is your young man into cars, Tara?

GERALDINE: Well he must be, darling, if he's an engineer.

PAUL: Not necessarily, darling ...

TARA: No, he loves cars ...

PAUL: Good, then I will insist on showing him what I have
             out there – the new Land Rover, four-wheel drive,
             2.2 litre turbo-diesel engine, automatic transmis-
             sion – complete top-of-the-range job.

TARA: *(TOLERANTLY)* Oh lovely. *(AWKWARDLY)* Would
             you like to sit down, or something?

GERALDINE: Well, first, these *(THE CHOCOLATES)* are for your
             mam ... when she gets back.

TARA: Yes, she's still out walking ...

GERALDINE: And we have our camera for that special photo of
             you going off – and this *(THE ORCHID)* is for you
             for tonight.
             *(PAUL TAKES A SUDDEN FLASH-PHOTO – GER-
             ALDINE POSED, ARM AROUND TARA)*

GERALDINE: An orchid. For your dress.

TARA: *(POLITELY)* Oh, thank you.

GERALDINE: Not at all. Now, sit down here and tell me ... *(SITS)*

PAUL: *(DISAPPROVING, OF THE TROPHY)* Oh good
             God!

GERALDINE: *(ASKING 'WHAT'S THE MATTER')* What is it, dar-
             ling?

PAUL: *(INDICATES THE TROPHY)* A very good quest-
             ion.

GERALDINE: *(POLITELY)* Oh yes. *(EXCITED, TO TARA)* And
             now – nice, is he?

TARA: Who?

GERALDINE: Your student engineer.

TARA: Oh yes, he's brilliant.

PAUL: Doesn't play golf, does he?

GERALDINE: *(MERRILY TO TARA)* Oh don't start him of on golf
             either – do you know about the Japanese Four-Ball
             next March – did your mother tell you?

TARA: The Japanese what?

PAUL: Oh it's just some executives from our parent com-
             pany in Japan who are coming over ...

GERALDINE: And he's gone all monastic in preparation ...

PAUL: I'm not darling – I'm playing my regular game – as
             I will do in the Japanese Four-Ball ... *(TO TARA)* ...

	as I may do with your young man, if he indulges in the odd round or two?
TARA:	Actually he doesn't play golf at all – just rugby in the winter and cricket in the summer.
GERALDINE:	Oh lovely, very nice. And this is serious, is it? I mean have you both discussed ... you know ... *(HER WEDDING-RING FINGER)*
TARA:	Oh, well yes, eventually, I suppose – the only problem is he's already applied for a post-grad. job in either Uruguay or Brazil.
GERALDINE:	Oh no!
PAUL:	Engineers to tend to travel, darling.
GERALDINE:	And would you really fancy Uruguay or Brazil?
TARA:	I haven't really made up my mind yet.
GERALDINE:	Well, I would because he sounds really dishy and travel does broaden the mind. We found that when we went on our first Caribbean cruise and spent two wonderfully exotic weeks in the Bahamas.
PAUL:	That was the Barbados, darling.
GERALDINE:	Oh yes. *(TO TARA)* Well, they're all the same, aren't they.
	(DERMOT APPEARS ON THE STAIRS. HE HAS CHANGED INTO A SUIT AND CRAVAT, WITH READING GLASSES HANGING AROUND HIS NECK. HE CARRIES A BOOK)
DERMOT:	Geraldine, Paul – I didn't hear you come in. *(COMES DOWN)*
GERALDINE:	Dermot, aren't you looking well. *(KISSES)*
	(TARA GOES QUICKLY INTO THE KITCHEN TO CHECK THE WATER, AS)
DERMOT:	And you, Geraldine ... and Paul, old pal.
PAUL:	Long time no see. *(SHAKES HANDS)*
DERMOT:	And all set for life on Jupiter?
PAUL:	Oh yes – send in the comets.
DERMOT:	We will at three-oh-seven A.M. – and a perfectly clear night for it – and you know, don't you, that I have been asked to take the official astronomical photo of the crash?
GERALDINE:	No – really?
DERMOT:	Oh yes, camera set up on my 6.25 scope and fully

computer linked ... oh, forgive me while I just ...
(THE COMPUTER HAS BLEEPED – AND DERMOT GOES TO IT, PRESSES A SERIES OF KEYS. A FAX BEGINS TO PRINT-OUT, ALL AS)
... some data being down-loaded for me. *(PRESSES MORE KEYS)* There we are. *(GOES TO THE FAX)* Yes, quite an honour to be selected, but a responsibility as well – *(OF THE FAX)* – ah, good wishes from my good friend Ahmed Al Sharood in Morocco – he says he'll be watching the crash in the company of his three favourite wives. Fascinating people.

GERALDINE: And we've been admiring your lovely house.

DERMOT: Yes, still beavering away on that ... re-hanging all the doors ... in the process of stripping them back to their natural pine ... and just finished completely re-flooring this entire room. *(STAMPS ON THE FLOOR. THE SHELF THAT SLIPPED BEFORE, NOW SLIPS AGAIN. ALL TURN TO LOOK AT IT. QUICKLY)* And just a shelf or two to be looked-at. Sit down, please, sit down. *(AS THEY SIT)* So Paul, how's the golf? – I hear you have a big game coming up.

PAUL: Oh yes, the Japanese Four-Ball: yes, we'll need to make a big impression on that day – but we're confident, very confident indeed.

GERALDINE: The company now see Paul as their key player ...

PAUL: Well, the handicap is now safely in single figures – however, I heard recently that I'll be going out with Mr Sakamoto who is now not only their Chief Executive but a nine-handicapper to boot. *(TO DERMOT)* Must try and get you out, Dermot, now that you have time on your hands.

DERMOT: The problem being, Paul, I'm busier than ever.
(PAUL HAS PICKED UP THE 'PLACED' BOOK AND READ THE COVER)

DERMOT: *(TAKES THE BOOK)* Oh let me take that out of your way – I don't know who could have put that there. *(AS TARA COMES ANGRILY FROM THE KITCHEN)* Ah Tara, is your mother still out?

TARA: *(SWEETLY)* Still walking in the moonlight.

DERMOT: And the water?
TARA: *(HUSHED)* Still freezing!
DERMOT: *(COVERING-UP)* Ah good, excellent. Take Gerald-
             ine's coat, Tara.
GERALDINE: Well, I was going to ... (keep it on for a while)
DERMOT: Not cold, are you?
GERALDINE: *(TAKES IT OFF. COLD)* Oh, no no – not at all. Thank
             you, Tara.
             *(TARA TAKES GERALDINE'S COAT, HANGS IT
             QUICKLY IN THE HALL-WAY, AS GERALDINE
             SITS, NOW VERY COLD. TARA RETURNS QUICK-
             LY, INTENT ON GETTING UPSTAIRS, WITH HER
             ORCHID, AS)*
DERMOT: Now, what can I get you? Geraldine?
GERALDINE: A sherry would be lovely.
DERMOT: Absolutely. *(SEEING TARA TRYING TO ESCAPE
             UPSTAIRS)* A moment, Tara! *(TARA STOPS)* Paul,
             are you still ...?
PAUL: Mineral water would be fine.
DERMOT: Oh you still can't ...?
PAUL: No, no – I can take it or leave it anytime I like.
DERMOT: I'm really delighted to hear that.
PAUL: Doesn't bother me either way now.
DERMOT: You'll try a small whiskey then ...?
PAUL: No, honestly, a mineral water would be fine.
DERMOT: Maybe later. *(AS TARA GOES AGAIN)* Could you
             bring in some ice, Tara?
GERALDINE: *(COLD)* Not for me, Dermot.
PAUL: *(COLD)* Or me.
DERMOT: Sure?
PAUL: Absolutely.
DERMOT: The ice is not necessary, Tara.
TARA: *(HARD)* No kidding.
             *(TARA GOES. A BRIEF SILENCE FALLS, AS DER-
             MOT GETS THE DRINKS. THEN)*
GERALDINE: Lovely to see her growing up so well – from god-
             child to debutante.
DERMOT: Oh Tara? Yes – she's really blossomed up here.
GERALDINE: It is magnificent. And the silence, Paul?
PAUL: What a silence – we were saying out there that we

never heard anything like the silence out there.

DERMOT: It's what people come to hear. The silence. And the stars, of course.

PAUL: Yes, magnificent spectacle.

DERMOT: Closer to comet-time – from about 2.30am – I'll give you a complete run-down on the whole firmament and, while I'm photographing the actual crash, you can observe Jupiter and, of course, its Galilean satellites of Io, Europa, Ganymede and Collisto.

PAUL: Look forward to that.

DERMOT: *(WITH THE DRINKS)* Now – a sherry, Geraldine ...

GERALDINE: Oh ta.

DERMOT: Mineral water for Paul ...

PAUL: Cheers.

DERMOT: And a brandy for my good self. Your good health. *(ALL DRINK. THEN SILENCE. THEN AWKWARD-LY)*

DERMOT: Stella won't be long.

PAUL: Oh good. *(THEN)* And as soon as she arrives, we have something to show you. A little surprise.

GERALDINE: A blast from the past, Dermot.

PAUL: I'll just get our bag from the car.

DERMOT: Oh excellent. Great. Look forward to that. Yes. *(PAUL GOES. SILENCE. THEN)*

GERALDINE: *(TO DERMOT, AWKWARDLY)* And there's that lovely silence again.

DERMOT: Oh yes.

GERALDINE: I could listen to it all night.

DERMOT: You probably will. *(REALISES)* In bed, I mean – not down here. Down here, we'll all be chatting away non-stop but when you're in bed and it's quiet, it'll come creeping in. *(GERALDINE LOOKS OVER. CORRECTS)* The silence, I mean, will come creeping in. Nothing else. It's quite safe up here. Totally safe, in fact – it's what we love about country life: no fear, no burglar alarms, no police sirens, just peace of mind. And I think you'll enjoy your bedroom too – and the Velux windows: let you see the stars as you lie there – nature at its most spectacular.

116

GERALDINE: And it's a double, is it?

DERMOT: Pardon me?

GERALDING: No no, nothing.

(PAUL COMES IN. HE CARRIES A TRENDY OVER-NIGHT BAG. WE NOTICE THAT HE HAS PUT ON A SCARF UNDER HIS JACKET)

PAUL: Is that your wagon I see out there, Dermot?

DERMOT: *(HOPEFULLY)* Who, Stella? Is she coming?

PAUL: No – your wagon, your car.

DERMOT: Oh my car? Oh yes. Just for going into town.

PAUL: What is she – a four-wheel or a two-wheel?

DERMOT: *(AMUSED)* It's a car, Paul – they all have four wheels.

PAUL: *(SERIOUSLY)* No, drive – two-wheel drive or four-wheel drive.

DERMOT: *(SERIOUSLY)* Oh right. Two. Two-wheel drive. The front two I think or maybe the back. Never really looked to be honest.

PAUL: Should think of a four – especially for these roads. Give it some thought.

DERMOT: Oh right.

PAUL: And correct me if I'm wrong, but do I recognise that swivel chair?

DERMOT: Which, Paul?

PAUL: That chair – very like the one you had in the old office – the one you used slide around in.

DERMOT: Oh really, is it?

PAUL: And the desk – very like the old stuff we threw out in our de-layering of the company.

DERMOT: Yes, I suppose it is.

PAUL: But it's not, is it? ... from the old office ...?

DERMOT: Oh no no ...

PAUL: It's very like it. *(MERRILY)* I can almost see you sitting there, eating your Marietta biscuits. You don't still eat those, do you?

DERMOT: You must be joking. I've left all that behind.

PAUL: *(TO GERALDINE)* We used to think he had shares in Marietta biscuits. *(SITS)*

DERMOT: All a thing of the past. *(THEN, MOCK CASUALNESS)* And how is the job now anyway, Paul –

	things going well there, since the restructuring?
PAUL:	Oh very stream-lined now – you wouldn't recognise it.
DERMOT:	Good. And the Unions?
PAUL:	No trouble anymore.
DERMOT:	*(LIGHTLY)* Not like when you were the Union Rep? *(TO GERALDINE)* Those days he gave the Company hell – now I bet he gives the Unions hell.
PAUL:	*(SERIOUSLY)* Except that it's not quite like that in business anymore, is it? – today the focus is on Company viability in a European context – and that generates an on-going commitment that runs right through from their Trade Union agenda to our Management Structure and, on an individual level, from the Company Manager right down to our office boy.
DERMOT:	*(WEAKLY)* Oh right.
	(SHORT AWKWARD SILENCE)
GERALDINE:	I presume you know him.
DERMOT:	The office boy?
GERALDINE:	No, Tara's escort.
DERMOT:	Oh – no, I haven't actually met him but I hear he's a terrific fellow, very popular by all accounts.
GERALDINE:	And an engineer?
DERMOT:	Oh yes, only the best for Tara.
GERALDINE:	I always knew Tara would do wonderfully well.
DERMOT:	Absolutely. And there's something else: you'll have no trouble remembering his name. Believe it or not, it's ... Sean Connery. *(REALISES. CORRECTS)* No no, not Sean Connery ... it's ... you know ... 'Some Like It Hot'.
GERALDINE:	*(OF THE COLD)* No no, we're fine, really, we're fine.
DERMOT:	No, the film, 'Some Like It Hot' – his name is the same as the film-star in that.
PAUL:	Jack Lemmon?
DERMOT:	No – the other one.
GERALDINE:	Marilyn Monroe?
DERMOT:	What? No no – Tony Curtis!
GERALDINE:	Oh.
DERMOT:	Yes – just think of that film and you have it.

GERALDINE: Oh yes, right. *(THEN)* And they could finish-up in either Uruguay or Brazil?

DERMOT: Who could?

GERALDINE: Tony Curtis and Tara.

DERMOT: *(LOST)* Why's that?

GERALDINE: Because she just said so – after he graduates.

PAUL: Now you've worried Dermot.

DERMOT: *(TRYING TO BE LIGHT)* No no, whatever they want to do is all right with us.

(ANOTHER AWKWARD SILENCE. THEN)

DERMOT: Hard to believe – as we're sitting here, chatting away, that comet is thundering through space at an unstoppable 100,000 miles a minute heading to smash into Jupiter with the force of ten nuclear explosions – and there is nothing that Jupiter can do about it.

PAUL: Absolutely staggering thought.

(TARA COMES DOWN THE STAIRS, NOW IN HER DRESSING-GOWN, READY FOR HER BATH. SHE IS AGITATED)

TARA: Excuse me, daddy – is mum not back yet?

DERMOT: Not yet, love.

TARA: Do you know where the big enamel bucket is?

DERMOT: The big enamel bucket? What do you want that for?

TARA: *(ANNOYED)* Dad, Mum will be looking for it – do you know where it is?

DERMOT: It's out the back – I put the manure in it for the roses.

TARA: *(ANGRILY)* Oh Christ!

(TARA GOES TEARFULLY. DERMOT LOST)

GERALDINE: Is she all right?

DERMOT: Oh yes – teenagers. *(SILENCE. THEN)* The man behind it all is, of course, Harold.

PAUL: Pardon?

DERMOT: Dr Harold Metcalf, one of the most brilliant astronomers on the Net – and believe it or not, he still lives with his mother in Norwich, but what a mind. It was Dr Harold who personally selected me to take the official photographs tonight.

GERALDINE: Really? *(POLITE QUESTION)* What I often wonder about astronomers, Dermot, is have they com-

119

	pletely ruled out life out there – like are there really big, green, jelly-like aliens who might any day decide to visit us?
DERMOT:	It's a good question, Geraldine, and to answer it, we must consider the technology from NASA, the evidence of Hubble, the data from Space Station Mir, not to mention the recent revelations from Mars – and taking all into account, the scientific consensus is ... we just don't know.
GERALDINE:	Really? So it's possible that any day – or any minute – an alien could suddenly ... *(SCREAMS)* ... oh Jesus Christ!
	(THERE'S BEEN A SUDDEN CRASH AND STELLA HAS STAGGERED IN THROUGH THE CONSERVATORY DOOR. SHE CAN SEE VERY LITTLE. SHE WILL KNOCK OVER SOME FURNITURE. SHE LOOKS, IN A DIRTIED COAT AND WITH A DIRTIED FACE, AS THOUGH SHE HAS FALLEN IN MUD)
DERMOT:	Ah Stella, come in come in.
GERALDINE:	Is that you, Stella?
STELLA:	*(BLINDLY)* Yes, hello everybody – sorry I got delayed, Dermot.
PAUL:	Did you fall, Stella?
STELLA:	Oh just a stumble ... *(STUMBLES AGAIN)* ... nothing at all.
DERMOT:	*(GOES TO HER)* As you can see, Stella, Geraldine and Paul have arrived. *(POINTS QUIETLY)* Geraldine over there – Paul here..
STELLA:	Geraldine, don't kiss me until I ...
GERALDINE:	No no ... *(A SMALL HUG. QUIETLY)* I must talk to you.
STELLA:	What?
GERALDINE:	Later. *(LOUDLY)* And now, has Paul changed much?
DERMOT:	*(POINTS)* Over there.
STELLA:	Oh hello, Paul – long time no ... but don't ...
PAUL:	You try and stop me! *(KISSES HER)*
GERALDINE:	And we brought you some chocolates.
DERMOT:	*(INDICATES)* Over there.

STELLA:	*(DIMLY)* Aren't they lovely. Really Geraldine.
PAUL:	And an orchid for Tara to wear. *(INDICATES UP-STAIRS)*
STELLA:	*(PRETENDS TO SEE IT ON THE TABLE)* Oh it looks lovely.
DERMOT:	No, Tara took that upstairs.
STELLA:	*(ANNOYED)* Oh she did, did she! Please excuse me while I ... *(WALKS INTO SOME FURNITURE)*
PAUL:	Absolutely, Stella – then we have something to show you and Dermot.
GERALDINE:	A blast from the past.
STELLA:	Oh lovely. *(TURNS ON THE STAIRS)* Oh Dermot, do you know where the big enamel bucket is?
DERMOT:	Tara was saying you'd be looking for that.
STELLA:	Oh she has it, has she?
DERMOT:	No, it's out in the back with the manure in it.
STELLA:	Oh Christ! *(STAGGERS UP THE STAIRS AND OFF)*
PAUL:	Stella's looking well – I mean underneath all the ... eh ...
DERMOT:	Oh yes – she just loves walking.
PAUL:	And she didn't hurt herself, did she?
DERMOT:	Stella? Not at all – an odd stumble in the dark never bothers Stella or any of us. You come up any night and you'll find the three of us out there, walking along, falling down, getting up, laughing at it all in hail, rain or shine.
GERALDINE:	That's wonderful.
DERMOT:	Try doing that in the city – walking at night: if the muggers don't get you, the sex-maniacs will. There has to be more to life than that.
GERALDINE:	Very true. *(THEN)* Dermot, I have a wrap in our bag ... *(GOES TO IT)* You don't mind if I ...?
DERMOT:	You're not cold, are you?
GERALDINE:	*(FINDING IT)* Oh no no – just all the excitement of what you were saying and of seeing Tara going off and Jupiter and everything.
DERMOT:	Oh absolutely. And the rads are coming on nicely now – and we have an electric blanket on your bed, in case.
PAUL:	Oh good.

GERALDINE: It's a double, is it, Dermot?

DERMOT: Pardon me?

GERALDINE: Nothing. *(AS SHE TRIES TO GET WARM IN HER WRAP)* And what time is he due – Tony Curtis.

DERMOT: Oh anytime now. I think they're meeting up with a whole gang of them. Tara says he's really popular with all her friends.

GERALDINE: Isn't that wonderful. She must be so proud.

DERMOT: Oh she is. She mightn't often say it, but she is. And why not.

(AWKWARD SILENCE. A DOG BARKS, AWAY IN THE DISTANCE. THEN SILENCE AGAIN. THEN)

DERMOT: She's not our's, you know – we're just minding her for someone.

GERALDINE: Who – Tara?

DERMOT: Tara? No no, that dog you hear.

GERALDINE: Oh sorry.

DERMOT: We're minding her for our next-door neighbours who live four miles across the valley. The O'Mahony's.

GERALDINE: Oh.

DERMOT: Yes, that's something else about this life – the O'Mahony's can go away to Florida for three weeks and not a worry about who's minding the house, their property, their dog. In a word, it gives you peace of mind.

PAUL: And it doesn't get too lonely? – like, apart from the stars and that, is there anything else to do up here?

DERMOT: *(PROUDLY)* You mean apart from being in An Taisce, lobbying the Government to save the pine trees in Glen Valley, being a member of the Gun Club with a licence to own that double-barrelled chap over there ... *(INDICATES THE SHOT-GUN)* ... restoring this entire house, doing an Open University Degree Course and, pride of place *(DELICATELY PICKS UP THE TROPHY)* being the current holder of the All-Ireland Astronomy Quiz Trophy.

PAUL: *(NOT IMPRESSED)* They gave you that?

DERMOT: I won it. Two years running. Once more and it's mine.

GERALDINE: Isn't it beautiful?

PAUL: Beautiful is not the word.

GERALDINE: Yes it is.

DERMOT: All the planets are exact to the nearest centimetre and, it is all so delicately set, that no insurance company would touch it. Anyone want to hold it?

PAUL: Oh no thanks.

GERALDINE: Butter fingers.

DERMOT: *(REPLACES IT CAREFULLY)* Yes, I'm quite proud of that. (LIGHTLY) And apart from all that, Paul – no, I do nothing at all up here.

PAUL: *(LIGHTLY)* Point well taken and question withdrawn.

(GENERAL LAUGHTER AS STELLA COMES IN. SHE HAS CLEANED AND PUT HER CONTACT LENSES IN. SHE WEARS A CARDIGAN AGAINST THE COLD. IN TIME, WE WILL NOTICE THAT SHE IS UNCOMFORTABLE WITH THE LENS, OCCASIONALLY CAUSING HER TO WINK)

STELLA: Sorry about that, everybody.

DERMOT: You're fine, darling – everything all right? *(INDICATES HIS EYES)* Everything in and satisfactory?

STELLA: *(BLINKS)* Yes. Grand. And I found my glasses.

DERMOT: You're grand as you are. Now, a drink?

STELLA: Oh, a sherry, Dermot, please.

DERMOT: Good, very good. And Geraldine?

GERALDINE: I'm fine, thank you.

DERMOT: Paul?

PAUL: No thanks.

DERMOT: Sure?

PAUL: Absolutely.

(STELLA LOOKS AT DERMOT IN DISAPPROVAL)

DERMOT: Good, very good. *(GOES TO THE DRINKS)*

GERALDINE: *(TO STELLA)* We've just been admiring your lovely house.

STELLA: Oh, that's all Dermot.

PAUL: And, more important, how well you're looking – the country life certainly suits you.

STELLA: *(AWKWARD AT THE COMPLIMENT)* Thank you, Paul. And how are you – your golf and your handi-

123

cap and everything?

PAUL: The golf is going very well indeed, Stella – Geraldine may have told you about the up-coming Japanese Four-Ball.

GERALDINE: *(PROMPTS STELLA)* Yes, I did.

STELLA: Oh yes – against the Japanese. *(AS SHE TAKES HER SHERRY FROM DERMOT)*

PAUL: Which means my form is good, I'm now down to single figures and I am confident, on the big day, of getting out there and really kicking some ass.

GERALDINE: *(LIGHTLY)* I thought the purpose of golf was to hit the ball into the hole.

PAUL: *(SERIOUSLY)* The purposes of golf, darling, are manifold and one of them *is* hitting the ball – the others include a tactic which, you may remember, resulted in us winning the Sumatra Contract and in me getting that promotion that you liked so much.

GERALDINE: *(EXCITED, TO STELLA)* Oh yes, I couldn't believe it when he came home and ...

PAUL: It's a good story, Dermot: one of our rivals in the States was all ready to jump in and grab it – but, as luck would have it, Sumatra's head honcho happened to be in Ireland – I said I'd take him out on the course – a little wager: loser pays for the dinner and the drinks – all agreed and off we go. At the fourth I'm two down and I mention the Sumatra Contract – he's in good form, he's ahead so we chat on – at the seventh, I'm four down and he's telling me all about it, speaking really freely – at the eleventh I'm in the bunker and I casually mention what we can offer, give him a new ball-park figure, talk of flexibility and compromise and so forth – he's playing like Faldo so he's over the moon and now he makes a call on his mobile and suddenly we're talking serious business. On the thirteenth, we're back to all-square and he's thinking hard and playing harder – next green he goes one up again and we do the deal, shake hands and it's in the bag. And now, worries over, I turn on the heat, birdies and pars, he goes to pieces, and we're back in the

	club-house with the game, a free dinner, free drinks and the Contract all sown up. *(OF GERALDINE)* And some people still think that golf is all about hitting a ball into a hole.
DERMOT:	Amazing, isn't it.
PAUL:	And now I'm determined to get Dermot out, ASAP, just like old times.
GERALDINE:	Speaking of old times, Paul – our 'blast from the past'.
PAUL:	Oh yes – now, old timers, we want to check your memories here. Gather round.
GERALDINE:	*(EXCITED)* You're going to love this, Stella. come on sit here ... and you too Dermot.
	(PAUL HAS TAKEN A PHOTOGRAPH FROM THEIR BAG – IT'S THE SAME ONE AS STELLA HAD EARLIER)
PAUL:	Shove up in the bed there, Stella.
	(PAUL NOW JOINS THE OTHER THREE ON THE SETTEE, AND)
PAUL:	Now – who do you recognise in this photo?
STELLA:	*(REALISES)* Dermot, it's the Dinner Dance photo!
GERALDINE:	Do you have this one?
⎰DERMOT:	No!
⎱STELLA:	Yes!
STELLA:	No no, I just remember it.
PAUL:	Ring a bell, does it, Dermot?
DERMOT:	*(PRETENDS IT'S SINKING IN)* Oh, yes ...
PAUL:	Their Bank's Dinner Dance.
DERMOT:	Oh, yes ...
PAUL:	*(TO STELLA)* Remember you said you had won two tickets and would I go with you?
STELLA:	I *had* won two tickets ...
PAUL:	I'm not saying anything! *(TO DERMOT)* And I went back to the office and asked you did you want to go with her mate, Geraldine.
GERALDINE:	*(MERRILY)* And being a gentleman he paid for the tickets – sweet Dermot.
PAUL:	And the band kept playing a dreadful thing called 'Stella by Gaslight' or something – you asked for it, Dermot ...

125

DERMOT:	Did I?
PAUL:	Don't deny it – 'Hey, her name is Stella – play Stella By Gaslight'. I thought you were drunk.
DERMOT:	I was drinking orange. But look at you.
PAUL:	*(DEFENSIVE)* No, that's just the way I was standing.
GERALDINE:	And look at my eye-shadow. *(GREAT LAUGHTER)* No wonder you didn't fancy me, Dermot.
DERMOT:	No, that's not why I didn't fancy you.
GERALDINE:	*(STOPS)* Oh, what was it then?
DERMOT:	No, I did fancy you.
GERALDINE:	*(MERRILY)* Liar – you fancied Stella.
DERMOT:	No I didn't.
STELLA:	Dermot!
DERMOT:	No – I did later.
GERALDINE:	And it was the week after that, that he *(PAUL)* asked me out.
PAUL:	Maybe I *was* drunk!
GERALDINE:	*(MERRILY)* Excuse me!
PAUL:	And this *(THE PHOTO)* was where it all began. *(THEY ALL PONDER THE PHOTO, NOSTALGIC-ALLY)*
PAUL:	And now, for the night that's in it, we thought it'd be nice to put it up somewhere.
DERMOT:	*(TRYING TO DEAL WITH THIS)* Great idea, Paul. If only we could find a place for it.
PAUL:	*(TAKES THE PHOTO)* Well what about here? *(PLACES IT IN FRONT OF DERMOT'S TROPHY)*
GERALDINE:	Oh that looks great, Dermot.
DERMOT:	*(RELUCTANTLY)* Yes, it does.
PAUL:	That was then – and now tonight, Tara is off to *her* Dinner Dance.
GERALDINE/STELLA:	Debs!
PAUL:	Oh excuse me!
TARA:	*(UPSTAIRS. SHOUTS ANGRILY)* Mum! Mum!
DERMOT:	*(CALLS)* Tara?
STELLA:	*(ANXIOUSLY)* Oh I know what she wants – I'll get it for her.
DERMOT:	You stay, Stella, I'll get whatever it is.
STELLA:	No Dermot, I can ...

DERMOT:	*(FIRM)* It's okay, Stella – I can handle it.
STELLA:	They're on the cooker, boiling, in saucepans.
DERMOT:	*(LIGHTLY, TO PAUL)* Women and Teenagers – we'll never understand them. *(GOING UPSTAIRS)*
PAUL:	Very true. Mind if I look at your telescope?
DERMOT:	Sure – use the small one – the big lad is set to photograph Jupiter.
PAUL:	Right.
DERMOT:	*(OF HIS DRINK)* Oh and maybe you'd hang onto my drink for me? *(GIVES IT TO PAUL)*
PAUL:	*(TAKEN ABACK)* What? Oh certainly.
STELLA:	Dermot!
DERMOT:	Back in a jiffy. *(GOES TO TARA)*
STELLA:	I'm terribly sorry, Geraldine ... *(TRIES TO TAKE THE DRINK FROM PAUL)* I'm so sorry, Paul ...
PAUL:	No, I can hold it for Dermot.
STELLA:	Absolutely not ... *(TAKES IT)* ... I'll leave it here for him.
PAUL:	Whatever you like – it's no problem. *(UNEASILY. THEN)* So, I'll have a look at Jupiter.
GERALDINE:	Do, darling, and I'll be joining you in a moment. *(PAUL GOES TO THE CONSERVATORY. HE WILL VIEW JUPITER THROUGH THE SMALLER TELESCOPE. HE WILL ALSO NOTICE THAT THE ROOM IS NOW WARMER AND WILL REMOVE HIS SCARF.*
	GERALDINE AND STELLA WILL SIT TOGETHER ON THE SETTEE. ALL AS)
STELLA;	I'm terribly sorry about that – I did warn Dermot ...
GERALDINE:	It's all right – there's worse things than that happening to me these days.
STELLA:	Oh? Is this what you wanted to tell me ... ?
GERALDINE:	It is – and, Stella, if ever I needed your help in this life, I need it now.
STELLA:	Why? What's wrong?
GERALDINE:	Well, first I put off going to the doctor ...
STELLA:	The doctor?
GERALDINE:	For tests, but I eventually went – and when he rang me at half-one today, I knew instinctively that the news was bad.

STELLA: Was bad?

GERALDINE: Stella, please don't keep repeating everything and winking at me like that ...

STELLA: *(PUTS A HAND OVER HER EYE)* Sorry, something in my eye.

GERALDINE: It makes me feel as if I'm telling you a joke when, in fact, it's the worst thing that could possibly happen.

STELLA: *(THE WORST)* Oh my God, Geraldine, you don't mean you've got ...?

GERALDINE: *(THEN)* Yes, pregnant.

STELLA: *(STOPS)* What?

GERALDINE: You heard me.

STELLA: *(RELIEVED)* But that's great – I thought you heard you were going to die of something.

GERALDINE: I'd be better off dying of something.

PAUL: *(LOOKING THROUGH THE TELESCOPE)* 'Beam me up, Scotty'.

STELLA: But you've always wanted a baby – for years you'd've given anything to be ... (pregnant)

GERALDINE: Will you keep your voice down!

STELLA: He doesn't know?

GERALDINE: It's not his.

STELLA: It's not his?

GERALDINE: You're at it again! *(STELLA PUTS HER HAND BACK)* It shouldn't have bloody happened – but you know Dave I told you about, our new counter clerk from Galway.

STELLA: Oh the very young fellow with the dark curly hair that you said must have a lovely body?

GERALDINE: Yes yes, him. *(THEN)* Well he has.

STELLA: Oh God.

GERALDINE: And all because I, as his superior, stupidly went back to his flat to look at some banking system he said he devised and would like to show me.

STELLA: Oh say no more. I mean, go on.

GERALDINE: And there I was sitting with this gorgeous fellow, young enough to be my son, looking at a stupid banking system – and suddenly, and he was absolutely cold sober, he suddenly began to say that, while I was with him, he was finding it very diffi-

128

	cult to control himself ...
STELLA:	God.
GERALDINE:	And eventually he ... well, to put it bluntly, he ...
STELLA:	Yes?
GERALDINE:	... well ... eventually he ... didn't.
STELLA:	He didn't? So how are you pregnant?
GERALDINE:	He didn't control himself!
STELLA:	Oh!
PAUL:	*(AT THE TELESCOPE)* 'It's life, Jim, but not as we know it.'
GERALDINE:	*(TO STELLA)* So, after years of nothing ever happening, that young-fellow had only to look at me and I'm pregnant and soon I'll be as fat as ... as ... *(ALMOST INDICATES STELLA)* ... as I don't-know-who ... and Captain Kirk over there *(PAUL)* will then know for sure that it's not his. *(THEN)* We haven't for months. Years. We have separate everything.
STELLA:	Beds?
GERALDINE:	Rooms.
STELLA:	God.
GERALDINE:	All he needs is his golf, his job and his sleep. And ever since he went off the drink, I don't even get a 'goodnight darling' anymore. So thanks be to God we're here tonight because now what I'm depending on happening is
STELLA:	*(REALISING)* Oh God!
GERALDINE:	Will you just listen!
STELLA:	Yes, sorry.
GERALDINE:	So I'm depending on there being just a double bed in that room you've given us tonight. Is there, Stella?
STELLA:	A double bed? Yes – with an electric blanket.
GERALDINE:	Never mind the electric blanket – but what I want you to do, and I ask you this as a very old friend, I want you to insist on the two of us sleeping together tonight.
STELLA:	You and me?
GERALDINE:	For God's sake, Stella – me and Paul!
STELLA:	Oh yes, right. But how can I insist ...?
GERALDINE:	Just don't offer him another bed anywhere else.
STELLA:	Oh right – *(NERVOUSLY)* and then tonight you're

	going to try to get him to ... to ...?
PAUL:	*(AT THE TELESCOPE)* 'To boldly go where no man has gone before.'
GERALDINE:	To do anything – even a goodnight kiss ... and I might need time, Stella, so we may go to bed before Jupiter and then back again after it.
STELLA:	Yes, whatever you like – Dermot can set the alarms for you.
GERALDINE:	That'd be great. *(THEN)* And about offering him a drink ...
STELLA:	Oh I won't – and I'm sorry about Dermot ...
GERALDINE:	No, better if you do – maybe later and maybe not too much or he'll be like a raging bull – just enough to loosen him up.
STELLA:	And what about the Japanese Four-Ball?
GERALDINE:	To hell with the Japanese Four-Ball. Just see what you can do – I'll leave it up to you.
STELLA:	*(RELUCTANTLY)* Oh right.
GERALDINE:	Stella, I can't do it or he'd get suspicious ...
STELLA:	*(AGREEABLY)* Oh he would.
GERALDINE:	But not a word to Dermot ...
STELLA:	Oh no.
GERALDINE:	And hopefully. You should see the kind of nightdress I bought.
STELLA:	You poor thing.
PAUL:	*(AT THE TELESCOPE)* I could look at this all night.
GERALDINE:	*(TO STELLA)* And even with all that, it's not going to be easy. Just don't let me down ...
STELLA:	I won't.
GERALDINE:	Good. Now, better get him into some kind of mood. *(TAKES OFF HER WRAP. GOES TO PAUL)* All right, darling, my turn at the telescope. Push over.
STELLA:	*(TO HERSELF)* Christ!
PAUL:	*(STERNLY)* Geraldine, take it easy – there's no need to crawl all over me.
GERALDINE:	Sorry, darling. Now, is it set on Jupiter or do I move it or is it in position or what?
PAUL:	*(CURTLY)* You just look into it.
	(GERALDINE AND PAUL ARE SHARING THE SAME CHAIR – SHE LOOKING THROUGH THE

TELESCOPE, BEING AFFECTIONATE TO PAUL.
DERMOT COMES IN, UNNOTICED BY GER-
ALDINE AND PAUL)

DERMOT: *(QUIETLY)* Stella, Stella – everything all right?

STELLA: *(QUIETLY)* Oh yes, fine. Does Tara want the sauce-pans?

DERMOT: *(QUIETLY)* No she doesn't want the saucepans be-cause all the radiators are pumping hot, as I pre-dicted, and she's in the shower.

STELLA: *(FEELING VERY HOT)* Oh thank God, I thought it was me – I thought I was running a temperature. *(FEELS THE RADIATOR. CRIES OUT. IT IS ROAST-ING)*

DERMOT: See? *(OF TARA)* And she wants no one to let the engineer in except her.

STELLA: All right. And Dermot, Geraldine was saying she's a bit tired and she might go to bed before the comet-crash and come down to see it.

DERMOT: And is she bringing his nibs with her?

STELLA: Oh yes.

DERMOT: Good – because he's a bloody curse to try and talk to.

STELLA: And Dermot, I'd really like to change from these contact lenses ...

DERMOT: No no, you're fine, you're fine *(LOUDLY)* Well, Paul, still star-gazing?

PAUL: *(STANDS)* Not since I let this one at it.

DERMOT: Always the way. *(TAKES DOWN A LARGE EN-CYCLOPAEDIA)* But what I would now suggest is, when you decide to go to bed, you take this with you – get the whole background on how Jupiter was formed.

GERALDINE: *(STANDS)* Oh no!

STELLA: *(AWARE)* Dermot, I don't think Paul wants to ...

PAUL: No, I'd love to, Stella.

DERMOT: Of course. And Geraldine, for you *(A SMALLER ENCYCLOPAEDIA)* A short introduction to our Solar System. You'll find it invaluable before, dur-ing, or after, the crash.

GERALDINE: *(COLDLY)* Thank you, Dermot.

(IN THE DISTANCE, A DOG BARKING. THEN THE SOUND OF A CAR AND THE HEADLIGHTS SWEEP ACROSS THE CONSERVATORY. ALL VERY EXCITED NOW)

PAUL: *(EXCITED)* Hey Dermot – a car!

DERMOT: Oh great. That has to be Tara's boy.

STELLA: *(ANXIOUSLY)* But is Tara still in the shower ...?

DERMOT: *(EXCITED)* Stand-by everybody to interface.

GERALDINE: We should all be casual. *(SITS)*

PAUL: Get the camera ready.

DERMOT: *(CALLS)* Tara, I think your young man has arrived.

STELLA: Dermot, she wants to let him in.

DERMOT: I know! *(CALLS)* Tara, he's here.

TARA: *(OFF)* I'm in the shower, dad – put him in the kitchen – I'll be down in a minute.

DERMOT: Right. *(TO ALL)* Poor Tara, she thinks we'll say the wrong thing. Put him in the kitchen!

GERALDINE: She's anxious, poor thing.

PAUL: No worries – we'll do her proud.
(THE DOOR-BELL RINGS)

DERMOT: There he is. The moment has arrived. *(GOES)*

GERALDINE: Isn't this exciting?

PAUL: I won't take any photos until he settles in.

GERALDINE: *(EXCITED)* We should all be very casual – chatting. *(TRIES TO APPEAR CASUAL)*

DERMOT: *(OFF)* Come in, son, come in.
(STELLA AND GERALDINE WHIP AROUND TO WATCH THE DOOR)

DERMOT: *(OFF)* Come in, Tony, come in, meet everybody.
(DERMOT PROUDLY ENTERS. WITH HIM IS TARA'S ESCORT – HE IS 20, TALL, THIN, WITH HIS HAIR TIED BACK IN A PONY-TAIL. AWKWARD AND SLIGHTLY UNTIDY, EVEN IN HIS DRESS SUIT. HIS NAME IS TOMMY ... ALTHOUGH INITIALLY CALLED 'TONY' BY ALL. WE WILL RE-FER TO HIM AS 'TOMMY' THROUGHOUT)

DERMOT: This, everybody, believe it or not, is Tony. I was just thinking that the days when engineers looked like engineers are over. Great to see you, son – and now, this is my wife, Stella.

STELLA:	Very pleased to meet you, T (SHAKES HANDS)
TOMMY:	Pleased to meet you.
DERMOT:	And this is Geraldine and Pa
GERALDINE:	(SHAKES HANDS) Hello.
TOMMY:	Pleased to meet you.
PAUL:	(SHAKES HANDS) Good to mee you, Tony.
TOMMY:	(SHYLY) Hello.
DERMOT:	Sit down, sit down, Tony.
TOMMY:	Thanks. (SITS ON THE SETTEE, BETWEEN STELLA AND GERALDINE)
DERMOT:	Great. (CONFIDENTLY) Now Tony, t put you in the picture: Geraldine and Paul are old friends of ours – Geraldine and Stella worked together in the bank.
GERALDINE:	I still do, for my sins, Tony.
DERMOT:	Stella is luckier – once I retired, she packed it in and now spends her days relaxing up here in the beautiful Wicklow hills.
STELLA:	(WEAKLY) Yes.
PAUL:	(TO TOMMY) However, I'm still working in …
DERMOT:	(CUTS HIM OFF) Paul and I, on the other hand, used to be colleagues at work – Paul is still there and very successful, having once been a Trade Union representative until he went over to the company's side and was instantly promoted – say no more, Tony.
PAUL:	(ANNOYED) Just a minute, Dermot …
DERMOT:	Only kidding, Paul. (TO TOMMY) Geraldine and Paul, together, are the god-parents of Tara and have always been very caring towards her as they had neither sons or daughters of their own.
PAUL:	Dermot, that's not the only reason we …
DERMOT:	Course not, Paul, course not. (TO TOMMY) And Tara won't be long – so, while you're waiting, perhaps something, perhaps something to drink?
TOMMY:	Glass of water?
DERMOT:	(MERRILY) Water? Hey, I know all about you kids and water – you're not on Ecstasy Tablets, are you?
TOMMY:	Why, how many do you want?
	(DISBELIEF AS DERMOT AND PAUL, GERALDINE

	AND S^LLA CONSIDER THIS. THEN TOMMY
	SUDD^LY LAUGHS. NOW, GREAT RELIEF AND
	MER^lENT FROM ALL THE ADULTS)
DERMOT:	*(LA^lIS)* How many do I want! Oh very good. Wa^l coming up, Tony. Sherry Geraldine?
GERALDINE:	Pl^le, Dermot.
DERMOT:	A^l you'll stay on the wagon, Paul?
STELLA:	^l, he might have something – will you, Paul?
PAUL:	^lhat? *(PUZZLED. MORE SO AS STELLA WINKS UNCOMFORTABLY WITH HER CONTACT LENS. THEN)* No no, mineral water will be fine, thanks.
DERMOT:	Yes, why not – the night that's in it. You'll have a small one.
PAUL:	No thanks …
DERMOT:	Or a brandy perhaps …
PAUL:	No …
DERMOT:	… vodka, Baileys, creme-de-menthe …?
PAUL:	A mineral water would be fine, thanks!
DERMOT:	Maybe later. You all right as you are, Stella?
STELLA:	I was thinking I might switch to a vodka and white perhaps?
DERMOT:	*(STOPS)* Sorry?
STELLA:	*(WINKS UNCOMFORTABLY AGAIN)* Just one, perhaps, if that's all right?
DERMOT:	*(THEN PUZZLED)* O–kay. And a brandy for my good self. *(DERMOT GETS THE DRINKS. PAUSE)*
GERALDINE:	And you're thinking about Uruguay, Tony, are you?
TOMMY:	What?
GERALDINE:	Or is it Brazil you were thinking of?
TOMMY:	I wasn't thinking of anywhere.
GERALDINE:	You're staying on in Ireland, are you?
TOMMY:	Yeah – why not?
GERALDINE:	Oh Tara will be delighted.
PAUL:	Tony, this way. *(A FLASH AS PAUL TAKES A PICTURE OF TOMMY. HURTS TOMMY'S EYES – AND STELLA'S)* We'll get some of the two of you later.
DERMOT:	All right, drinks, folks: sherry Geraldine, mineral water Paul, plain water Tony, just the one vodka for Stella …

STELLA:	*(QUIETLY, OF HER EYE)* Dermot before the photographs, I'd really like to … (change this lens)
DERMOT:	*(QUIETLY)* You're grand. *(LOUDLY)* And a brandy for my good self.
TOMMY:	*(FEELING HOT)* Boiling in here, isn't it?
GERALDINE:	*(SWEETLY)* It is *now*, Tony, yes.
DERMOT:	*(RAISES HIS GLASS)* Cheers everybody – to Tara and Tony.
ALL:	To Tara and Tony. *(DRINKS)*
TOMMY:	Thanks very much – and it doesn't really matter, but my name isn't Tony, it's Tommy.
DERMOT:	*(STOPS)* Pardon me?
TOMMY:	My name – youse all keep calling me Tony but it's Tommy.
STELLA:	Tommy? You mean your name's not Tony Curtis?
TOMMY:	No, I'm Tommy Carney.
DERMOT:	Tommy Carney? Then who's Tony Curtis?
TOMMY:	*(AMUSED)* He's a film star, isn't he?
STELLA:	But it's a Tony Curtis who's taking Tara to her Debs.
PAUL:	Her name is Tara Hudson … were you taking a Tara Hudson?
TOMMY:	Tara, yeah, that's her.
DERMOT:	*(TO TOMMY)* You *are* at the right house, are you?
TOMMY:	I think so. *(AMUSED)* Well it's the only one up here for miles, isn't it?
PAUL:	But you're not Tony?
TOMMY:	No – Tommy – not that it matters.
DERMOT:	*(STERNLY AND AUTHORITATIVE)* Believe me, it matters if our daughter is expecting a chap called Tony and instead a fellow called Tommy turns up …
GERALDINE:	But you are an engineer, aren't you?
TOMMY:	A what?
	(TARA LOOKS IN FROM THE STAIRS. SHE WEARS A DRESSING-GOWN, BUT SEEMS ALMOST READY OTHERWISE)
TARA:	*(CONCERNED)* Tony, what are you doing here?
TOMMY:	I'm taking you to the Debs, amn't I?
TARA:	No, in here – I told dad to put you in the kitchen.
DERMOT:	Tara, I'd like to ask you a few questions.
TARA:	Oh dad, you haven't been asking Tony questions,

	have you?
DERMOT:	First of all his name is not Tony, it's Tommy.
TARA:	What? *(TO TOMMY)* Sarah said your name was Tony – your real name.
TOMMY:	No, Tommy ... though hardly anyone knows that because everyone just calls me ...
TARA:	*(QUICKLY)* Yes I know what we call you – and never mind that now. Did you get a car?
TOMMY:	There was none left in the garage so I took the hearse.
DERMOT:	A hearse?!
TARA:	*(DELIGHTED)* Oh my God! You're not serious! Did you?
TOMMY:	*(MERRILY)* Certainly I did. Mate of mine wanted to get a coffin for you to get into.
TARA:	I'm not getting into any coffin.
TOMMY:	No, we couldn't get one.
TARA:	Good. Give me two minutes, Tony.
TOMMY:	Tommy.
TARA:	Sorry 'Tommy'. You didn't mention your other name, did you?
TOMMY:	No – my mate said that Sarah said that you said I was only to give my real name to your oul fella ... *(CORRECTS)* ... to your father.
TARA:	Good, that's fine – and did she give you any other messages?
TOMMY:	About what?
TARA:	*(ANXIOUSLY)* Don't say another thing, to anyone. I'll be back in a minute. *(ANGRILY)* I asked for Tony to be shown into the kitchen, not in here! *(TARA GOES QUICKLY)*
DERMOT:	A hearse? *(RUNS OUT THROUGH THE ENTRANCE DOOR TO CHECK)* *(STELLA LOOKS AT TOMMY AND HE CATCHES HER EYE WINKING. FIRST PUZZLED, THEN MISUNDERSTANDS THIS)*
TOMMY:	Howya.
STELLA:	*(PUTS HER HAND OVER ONE EYE)* Excuse me, Tommy, but do you know Tara very long?
TOMMY:	Well yeah – like my mate goes out with her mate so

136

I see her coming from school though, up to now, we've usually only slagged each other as she goes by.

DERMOT: *(COMES QUICKLY IN)* Holy Christ – there *is* a hearse outside. The biggest one I ever saw in my life. I thought he was joking. Stella, look!
(DERMOT, STELLA, PAUL AND GERALDINE GO TO THE CONSERVATORY WINDOW TO SEE)

TOMMY: No, that's it, that's the one I came in – it goes like a bomb.

PAUL: Are you insured to drive that?

TOMMY: Why, who's asking?

DERMOT: *(STERNLY)* Well I am, for one – and I'm also asking did you seriously intend to get my daughter into a coffin?

TOMMY: No, not me, me mate did. He thought it'd be cool, pulling up to the hotel, her risin' up out of it like the Bride of Dracula.

DERMOT: Oh is that so?

STELLA: Dermot, I'll go and talk to Tara ... *(GOING)*

DERMOT: *(STERNLY)* Stella, you stay here – I'll talk to her ...

STELLA: *(MORE DETERMINED)* No, I'll talk to her.

DERMOT: *(HARD)* Stella, you stay here!

STELLA: *(SUDDEN ANGER)* No Dermot, I'm fed up with ... *(CONTROLLED)* Back in a minute.

DERMOT: Stella! *(LOUDER)* Stella!
(STELLA GOES UPSTAIRS. DERMOT FURIOUS AT HER)

PAUL: *(TO DEFUSE)* Dermot, I personally don't think we should make too much of this – it's Tara's big night out and what matter ...

DERMOT: Excuse me, Paul, I think I can handle it.

GERALDINE: I'd just like to know what kind of an engineer he is.

DERMOT: Well, let's start there. Tommy or Tony or whatever your name is, maybe you'd tell us what kind of an engineer you are or are you an engineer at all?

TOMMY: Are you serious?

DERMOT: I'm very serious.

TOMMY: *(AMUSED)* Well, I'm not really an engineer excepting that I do work *near* engines – in Nestors Garage

	in Terenure. I'm the puncture-fixer there.
DERMOT:	You're the what?
TOMMY:	I fix the punctures, on and off. Like when I'm off, I go on the dole – but I'm thinking of enrolling in a mechanic's course, but there's no rush.
GERALDINE:	So you're not an engineer at all?
TOMMY:	*(AMUSED)* No, but then neither is them train drivers in America and they all call themselves engineers.
PAUL:	*(LIGHTLY)* That's a good point.
DERMOT:	*(ANGRILY TO TOMMY)* And this other name you have, the one you're usually called – what is that, may I ask?
TOMMY:	Ah that's only a name I got years ago, because of what I'm into, and it sorta stuck and now everyone calls me it and I really ...
DERMOT:	Yes yes yes – but what is it?
TOMMY:	Needles.
DERMOT:	*(AGHAST)* Needles?
	(STELLA COMES DOWN THE STAIRS)
STELLA:	*(HAPPILY)* All right everybody – Dermot, I spoke to Tara and it's all worked out – and here she is, everybody, the belle-of-the-ball.
	(TARA COMES DOWN. SHE IS LOOKING BEAUTIFUL IN AN ELEGANT DRESS)
TARA:	*(DOES A TURN)* Da-daaaaaa.
GERALDINE:	Oh Tara, you look gorgeous.
	(ALL, EXCEPT DERMOT, APPLAUD. PAUL TAKES A PHOTO)
TOMMY:	*(GOING TO TARA)* Oh yes – very tasty.
STELLA:	And, Tommy, Tara will be travelling in the front seat of the hearse ...
TARA:	*(MERRILY)* No way was I ever getting into a coffin.
TOMMY:	*(MERRILY)* You would've if I got one – I don't take no for an answer.
TARA:	I'd rather die first! Get it? Coffin.
	(TOMMY, TARA AND STELLA ENJOY THIS JOKE)
STELLA:	And now, Paul, for their photo, I think they should hold our photo *(TAKES THE DINNER DANCE PHOTO)* just to show the difference.

PAUL:	Now that's a great idea. *(ORGANISING)* Tara, you sit here, Tommy behind you ... the photo in your hand, Tara ...
GERALDINE:	And everything is all right, Stella?
STELLA:	It's fine – I'll explain it all later. *(OF THE PHOTO)* Now Tara, who do you recognise there?
TARA:	*(WITH THE PHOTO)* Oh my God. Look Tony.
TOMMY:	Tommy.
TARA:	Tommy!
TOMMY:	*(LOOKS)* Jas, when was this? *(AMUSED, OF DERMOT)* Look at all the hair on your oul fella!
TARA:	*(AMUSED)* And mummy, you're not with dad?
STELLA:	No, I was with Paul then and Geraldine was with daddy.
TOMMY:	Oh-ho, know what you mean – say no more!
TARA:	Come on then – with the photo. I'll put on my funny face. *(PULLS A FACE)*
TOMMY:	Why when did you take it off?
TARA:	*(MERRILY HITS HIM)* Cheek of you.
	(DERMOT CAN TAKE NO MORE. WALKS IN BETWEEN PAUL AND TARA, SPOILING THE PHOTO)
PAUL:	For God's sake!
DERMOT:	*(HARD)* Excuse me, Tara – a moment if you please. *(TAKES HER HAND, LEADING HER ANGRILY TO THE KITCHEN)*
TARA:	*(PUTS THE PHOTO DOWN)* Dad, we're late already ...
DERMOT:	Late nor not, I want a word with you in private.
TARA:	*(GOING)* A word about what – we're having our photo taken ...
DERMOT:	There will be no photo and there will be no Debs dance either ...
	(THEY ARE NOW BOTH IN THE KITCHEN. ALL LISTEN, EMBARRASSED. STELLA WAITS AND THEN QUICKLY GOES INTO THE KITCHEN. THE ARGUMENT IS HOT AND HEAVY)
TARA:	*(OFF)* What?!
DERMOT:	*(OFF)* ... unless I get a suitable explanation ...
TARA:	*(OFF)* ... an explanation to what for God's sake?

139

DERMOT: *(OFF. FURIOUS)* Well for a start, as to who the hell he is and why you are going in a hearse or why we were told lies about him being an engineer on his way to Brazil.

STELLA: *(OFF)* Dermot, Tara explained how she ...

DERMOT: *(OFF)* And did she explain that he's an engineer who fixes punctures or why everyone calls him Needles ...

TARA: *(OFF)* Oh for God's sake!

DERMOT: *(OFF)* ... or why he drinks water or why he offered me Ecstasy Tablets ...

TARA: *(OFF)* I don't believe this!

DERMOT: *(OFF)* ... and thinking he can just walk in here out of a hearse and take my daughter away in a coffin.

TARA: *(OFF)* Dad, you have no right ...

DERMOT: *(OFF)* I have every right and if you'd told us who he was, we'd never have ...

TARA: *(OFF)* Oh I know you wouldn't because you are so bloody stuck-up in this house ...

DERMOT: *(OFF)* We are your parents – and we will decide ...

TARA: *(OFF)* And I've had enough of this ...

DERMOT: *(OFF)* Tara, don't you dare ...

(TARA COMES OUT, FOLLOWED BY DERMOT AND STELLA. THE ROW CONTINUES)

TARA: Dad, I know what you're doing ...

DERMOT: Yes, I'm telling you you're not ...

TARA: No, you're just trying to impress them ...

DERMOT: Tara, I will not have you talking like that in front of our guests ...

TARA: Why not? What are you afraid they'll hear?

DERMOT: *(QUIETLY ANGRY)* Keep your voice down ...

TARA: No dad – impress them all you like, but don't take it out on me the way you take it out on mum ...

DERMOT: I never take it out on anyone.

TARA: You do, you punish everybody because you were let go from your job ...

DERMOT: I was never let go!

TARA: ... and I'm sick and tired being made to suffer ...

STELLA: Tara!

DERMOT: When did you ever suffer ...?

140

TARA:	Being dragged up here, looking at you looking at stars, living like hermits, fifteen miles from my nearest friend and nothing to do but walk in fields full of sheep-shit and goat-shit.
DERMOT:	*(LOUDER)* That's it – now you are going nowhere. *(TO TOMMY)* I'm sorry sonny, but you are not taking my daughter to a Debs or anywhere else.
TARA:	Come on, Tommy, we're out of here ...
DERMOT:	Tara, sit down!
PAUL:	Dermot, the child's only going to a dance ...
DERMOT:	*(ANGRILY TO PAUL)* You know all about children, do you? How many have you got?
PAUL:	Christ, you were the same at the office ... no control, no common sense ...
DERMOT:	We're not in the office now!
TARA:	*(SEARCHING)* Tickets!
DERMOT:	Tara, you come back here.
	(THE FAX BEGINS TO PRINT-OUT)
PAUL:	For Christ sake, will you let her go if she wants to!
DERMOT:	Will you bloody-well mind your own business! Tara?
PAUL:	*(A HAND ON DERMOT'S SHOULDER)* Just calm down ...
DERMOT:	*(ANGRILY BRUSHES HIM OFF)* Get your hands off me!
STELLA:	Dermot!
TARA:	*(HAS FOUND THE TICKETS. GOING)* I'm going and I'm going in the back of the hearse!
DERMOT:	Tara, he's a bloody drug-pusher.
TARA:	*(LOUDLY AND PROUDLY TO ALL)* Come on, Needles!
	(TOMMY AND TARA GO QUICKLY)
DERMOT:	Tara, you come back here ...
STELLA:	Dermot, let me talk to her ... *(GOING)*
DERMOT:	*(HARD)* Stella, will you do what you're told and stay here – stay here and see to our guests ... even if they insist on interfering ... Tara? Tara! *(RUNS OFF)*
GERALDINE:	*(FOLLOWING DERMOT)* Stella, you stay – he's too angry. *(CALLS)* Dermot? Tara? *(FOLLOWS DERMOT)*

	(THE FAX STOPS. OUTSIDE, THE HEARSE HAS STARTED UP. A DOG BARKS. WE HEAR)
DERMOT:	*(OFF)* Tara, get out of that hearse this instant.
GERALDINE:	*(OFF)* Dermot, get out of the way or you'll be killed. *(A CAR HORN SOUNDS.*
	LIGHTS SWEEP ACROSS THE CONSERVATORY, AS THE HEARSE COMES NEAR AND DRIVES NOISILY OFF. THE VOICES FOLLOW, NOW FADING. THE DOG BARKS AWAY IN THE DISTANCE. ALL FADES.
	STELLA SITS WITH HER HAND TO HER FOREHEAD)
PAUL:	*(REMORSEFUL)* Jesus Christ, Stella – I shouldn't have butted-in like that ... that was none of my business ...
STELLA:	*(WEAKLY)* It's all right.
PAUL:	*(ANGRILY TO HIMSELF)* I just wish to Christ I wasn't watched all the time. Not that I need a drink – I don't, I honestly don't – but I'd be a lot calmer if everytime I even *looked* at a bottle, Geraldine didn't get another panic attack.
STELLA:	*(REMEMBERS)* What? Oh no, I don't think Geraldine would mind if you ...
PAUL:	Then you don't know Geraldine!
STELLA:	Well you can have one now if you wish.
PAUL:	*(LOOKS AT THE BOTTLES. DECIDES)* Thanks, Stella, but, no, I'm grand – they'll be back any minute anyway – no, I only wanted to *calmly* make the point that Tara was only going to a dance with the lad – *(NOW PICKS UP THE DINNER-DANCE PHOTO)* and Christ, I know it's ridiculous, but sometimes I can't help thinking of her as my own daughter.
STELLA:	Pardon?
PAUL:	No, I mean us – you and me – like in that photo, if we'd kept going out together ...
STELLA:	Paul ...
PAUL:	No, I know it's all in the past, but I did keep the photo, Stella, and everytime I look at it, I ... *(AS STELLA HOLDS HER HEAD)* Stella? Are you all

	right?
STELLA:	Yes yes – it's just a migraine.
PAUL:	A migraine? I don't ever remember you having migraines.
STELLA:	No, just recently I ... and I really shouldn't drink whenever I ... *(SMALL SMILE)* ... in fact, I think this is more vodka than migraine.
PAUL:	Christ I hate to see you like this. You were always so ...
STELLA:	I know – fat and funny.
PAUL:	What? No – you were high-spirited ... *(GENTLY)* ... you were lovely.

(DERMOT COMES ANGRILY IN. PAUL MOVES QUICKLY AWAY FROM STELLA. DERMOT WEARS HIS COAT. HE WILL NOW FIND HIS KEYS. GERALDINE WILL COME IN. ALL AS)

DERMOT:	That little bastard tried to run me down.
STELLA:	Where are you going?
DERMOT:	After them of course – and, by Jesus, if he stops the hearse and tries anything with Tara, I'll swing for him. *(TOWARDS PAUL)* And don't think I can't do this, don't think I can't take control of a situation.
PAUL:	*(CONTRITE)* I know you can, Dermot – and I want to say I'm very sorry for ...
DERMOT:	*(SEES THE FAXES)* When did these come in?
STELLA:	A minute ago while ...
PAUL:	Dermot, please, I just want to sincerely apologise for ...
GERALDINE:	Yes, we all do ...
DERMOT:	*(WITH THE FAXES)* Christ – faxes from the States and from London – and one from Harold, asking if I'm ready, have I seen it yet.
GERALDINE:	Seen what?
DERMOT:	Well hardly one of your green jelly-fish aliens – the comet! *(THEN)* Sorry, Geraldine, sorry – it's the bloody heat in this house. If you want to go to bed, I can set the alarms for 2.30 for Jupiter. Hopefully, I'll be back in time – and with Tara.
GERALDINE:	Yes Paul, maybe we will go to bed now.
PAUL:	Bed? At this hour?

	(DERMOT PICKS UP HIS SHOT-GUN AND CART-RIDGES)
STELLA:	Dermot, don't take that, please.
DERMOT:	Stella, that bastard's name is Needles, he's a drug-pusher, probably has a hypodermic ...
PAUL:	*(HARD)* Dermot, no, really I wouldn't.
DERMOT:	And the difference is, Paul, I would and, if he tries anything, I will. *(GOES)*
STELLA:	*(TO PAUL)* He's not a drug-pusher, is he?
PAUL:	*(LOOKS TO GERALDINE, UNSURE)* Eh, I wouldn't think so.
GERALDINE:	*(HOPEFULLY)* Of course he's not. And I don't think you should be worrying – Dermot will be back in no time. And meantime, you, all of us, should now try to get some sleep.
STELLA:	Pardon? *(REALISES GERALDINE'S AGENDA)* Oh yes, of course – I'll take you up to your bedroom ...
PAUL:	Bit early isn't it? *(LOOKS AT HIS WATCH)*
STELLA:	No no, Paul – we'll all need to get some rest –we have to be up again at half-two.
GERALDINE:	Exactly. Come on now, Paul.
PAUL:	Oh right.
	(OUTSIDE, THE SOUND OF DERMOT'S CAR AND LIGHTS SWEEP ACROSS THE CONSERATORY. ALL FADE, AS)
GERALDINE:	And our bedroom is where, Stella?
STELLA:	Oh yes, sorry – it's the one on the left of the stairs with the bed-side lamps and the Velux windows – I'll show you ...
GERALDINE:	We'll find it. And everything will be fine with Dermot and Tara and all that – you'll see.
STELLA:	Hopefully. I might just stay up a while and wait for Dermot.
GERALDINE:	Yes, do that. Come along, darling. *(GOES)*
PAUL:	Right. *(TURNS BACK)* Oh, must get my encyclopaedia, and yours ... do our homework.
	(PAUL PICKS UP THE ENCLYCOPAEDIAS, CHECKS THAT GERALDINE HAS GONE, THEN)
PAUL:	Stella, if you're staying up, I might drop down later.
STELLA:	Sorry, Paul?

PAUL:	Before Dermot gets back – for just a chat ...
STELLA:	What?
PAUL:	It's all right – Geraldine always takes a sleeping pill, even for a nap, and as soon as she nods off ...
STELLA:	No no, she won't be taking a pill tonight ...
PAUL:	A half one then – and as soon as she ...
STELLA:	No, no, Paul, you should stay with her ... *(GOES QUICKLY TO THE DRINKS WHERE SHE WILL POUR HERSELF ONE)*
PAUL:	For Christ sake, Stella – I'm only asking for a chat, about whatever you like: Dermot, Tara, you and Dermot, you and me, Jupiter, anything – we owe each other that at least.
STELLA:	*(PANIC)* No Paul, we don't owe each other anything.
PAUL:	Stella, will you relax!
STELLA:	But tonight ...
PAUL:	Please!
	(STELLA SITS, EXHAUSTED)
PAUL:	That's better. *(GENTLY MASSAGES HER SHOULDERS AND TEMPLES)* How do you feel?
STELLA:	Like bloody Jupiter.
PAUL:	What?
STELLA:	Nothing.
PAUL:	*(TENDERLY)* Stella, this is you, isn't it? – this is the part of you I always loved: poor Stella, wanting to let go but always afraid of what might happen. Maybe that's why you married old reliable Dermot instead of the danger of ...
STELLA:	*(ANNOYED)* Paul, that is not true and you have no right ...
PAUL:	*(GOOD HUMOURED)* Okay, sorry, just a joke – won't say it again. Promise. Okay, better go before Geraldine gets ideas, thinks I'm eyeing-up the bottles. *(PICKS UP HIS ENCLYOPAEDIAS)* So, see you later. Soon. And Stella, remember I always said I believed in fate ...?
STELLA:	Paul ...
PAUL:	... well, I honestly now believe that something great is going to come of this night. *(PAUSES TO STROKE*

HER CHEEK AS HE PASSES. NOW, AS HE GOES
UPSTAIRS, VERY SMOOTH, VERY CONFIDENT)
I do. Okay? Trust me.
(PAUL GOES. STELLA, RESIGNED AND IN DE-
SPAIR, SITS BACK ... AS WE FADE TO DARK-
NESS)

END OF ACT ONE

ACT TWO. SCENE ONE

FIRST, DARKNESS. STELLA IS ON THE SETTEE, HOLDING A DRINK, THINKING, DOZING. THEN GERALDINE APPEARS ON THE STAIRS, UNNOTICED BY STELLA.

GERALDINE: *(QUIETLY)* Stella? *(QUIETLY)* Stella. *(LOUDER)* Stella?

STELLA: *(NOW AWARE)* Oh Geraldine!
(LIGHTS UP. IT IS ONE HOUR LATER. THE ROOM IS AS BEFORE. GERALDINE WEARS A LONG, SILK AND SEXY, LOW-CUT NIGHT-DRESS. SHE CARRIES THE TWO ENCYCLOPAEDIAS)

GERALDINE: *(TENTATIVELY)* I don't want to disturb you if ...

STELLA: No, Geraldine – sorry, I was nodding off. *(THEN)* Is everything all right with your room?

GERALDINE: Oh the room's wonderful – I just wanted to leave these encyclopaedias back ...

STELLA: Oh yes – come in, come in.

GERALDINE: For just a moment – I won't stay long. Do you mind if I get myself a G&T?

STELLA: Oh of course not. *(THEN)* Where's Paul?

GERALDINE: *(GETS HER DRINK)* A very good question.

STELLA: Is he not in bed – I mean, have you managed to get him to ... ?

GERALDINE: I've managed nothing – ever since he found a pair of binoculars in a drawer and he's been sitting in the Velux window gazing at the stars for the past hour, while I'm draped across the bed in my new night-dress like a ... a ... a ... a

STELLA: I know – a prostitute.

GERALDINE: *(OFFENDED. THEN)* I was going to say 'like a bloody eegit'.

STELLA: *(ANXIOUSLY)* Yes, sorry sorry, I meant you were 'a bloody eegit.'

GERALDINE: No, you're right, I *am* like a prostitute up there – an ignored one at that.

STELLA: Oh Geraldine. *(THEN)* And I'm terribly sorry, I wasn't able to get him to drink anything ...

GERALDINE: Don't worry about it.

STELLA: Though I nearly did.

GERALDINE: It's that bloody Japanese Four-Ball. *(THEN)* I
smuggled those encyclopaedias back. I couldn't bear
it if he finished with the binoculars, took one look
at me and started on page one of that.

STELLA: Oh God, I know what you mean.

GERALDINE: It's a bloody nightmare, Stella, the whole thing.
This is my last chance and it's slipping away min-
ute by minute while he mopes around up there.
(THEN) You don't have any hints, do you?

STELLA: Me?

GERALDINE: Well you once went out with him.

STELLA: But that was nearly twenty years ago – and anyway we never ...

GERALDINE: *(KINDLY)* No, of course you didn't – I shouldn't
have asked: you were never like that.

STELLA: *(OFFENDED)* Pardon me?

GERALDINE: No, I mean you were never like me – you were never
one to really let yourself go.

STELLA: *(REALISES. OFFENDED)* Excuse me, Geraldine, I
often let myself go.

GERALDINE: Oh I'm sure you did but ...

STELLA: Just because I was a bit over-weight doesn't mean I
never had a chance to ...

GERALDINE: I never said you were over-weight.

STELLA: Geraldine, I *know* I was over-weight.

GERALDINE: No, you weren't.

STELLA: Of course I was and I still am.

GERALDINE: All right and so what if you are – I always wanted
to put on a few pounds ...

STELLA: No, you did not – but it still doesn't mean I never
let myself go ...

GERALDINE: ... Of course not ...

STELLA: ... and I still do ...

GERALDINE: *(FINALLY)* I know, that's what I'm saying – of
course you do because you have Dermot to let yourself go with!
*(STELLA LOOKS UP IN DESPAIR AT THE
NOTION, AS)*

GERALDINE: But if you went to Dave's flat like I did and there he was, looking gorgeous, half your age, cold sober, and fancying you like crazy, you'd still have run for your life, wouldn't you?

STELLA: *(WEAKLY)* Well I ...

GERALDINE: Of course you would because you're not like me. You don't have my life: the bank, the pressure, the social club, the tennis club, *(IRONIC)* the mixed doubles, the Health Club, the hairdressers, the lunches out with the girls, lunches out with the tennis club gang, back to the Health Club – the sauna, the reflexology, the aromatherapy – the endless golf-club do's, and the dinner-parties? – you go out to a *new* dinner-party and then you invite them back to *your* dinner-party, so they have to invite you to an even better dinner-party, so you invite them back to another dinner-party and then you all get together and go off to the Health Club to recover from all the bloody dinner-parties! Christ, the endless merry-go-round would drive you to do anything. *(STOPS. CALMLY)* That's why I envy you, Stella – it must be so dignified, you and Dermot.

STELLA: *(FLATLY)* Pardon me?

GERALDINE: I presume you both ...?

STELLA: Oh yes – and we really let ourselves go when we do.

GERALDINE: I meant sleep in the same bed.

STELLA: Oh yes. We do that too.

GERALDINE: So dignified – compared to all this carry-on. *(PAUSE)* God, it's roasting in here, Stella.

STELLA: *(ALSO ROASTING)* I know – I tried to turn off the heaters but ...

GERALDINE: No no, it's lovely ... it's grand. *(TRIES TO GET COOL, SOMEHOW – THE COLD GLASS AGAINST HER NECK, HER CHEST.*

SUDDENLY, IN THE FAR DISTANCE, A SHOT RINGS OUT. GERALDINE SURPRISED, STELLA HARDLY NOTICING. THEN)

GERALDINE: What was that?

STELLA: *(CASUALLY)* I don't know. Sometimes there are hunters out in the woods at night, usually illegal.

GERALDINE: Seems very far away. *(PAUSE. QUIETLY)* It's nice though, isn't it ... a sudden noise in all that silence.

STELLA: *(LISTENS)* Yes. I suppose so.

(A MOMENT OF QUIET REFLECTION – THEN THE SLIDING DOOR SLOWLY OPENS AND PAUL APPEARS. HE IS IN HIS TROUSERS, SHOES AND SHIRT, NOW WITH FIVE BUTTONS OPEN. GER-ALDINE, SEEING HIM, GUILTILY GIVES HER GLASS TO STELLA. PAUL, NOT SEEING GERALD-INE, QUIETLY CLOSES THE DOOR, TURNS AND ALMOST SLIDES DOWN THE REMAINING STEPS ON NOW SEEING HER)

PAUL: Oh! There you are, darling ...

GERALDINE: Paul! I just came down to get myself a hot drink of ... of ... cocoa and I found Stella waiting for Dermot so I was keeping her company.

PAUL: Oh good idea. *(AWKWARDLY)* Did anyone hear that bang?

GERALDINE: Stella says it's probably an illegal hunter.

STELLA: Out in the woods somewhere. *(STELLA INDICAT-ING, CLINKS THE TWO GLASSES, REALISES SHE HOLDS TWO, SHE DRINKS ONE AND PUTS IT ASIDE)*

PAUL: Ah very likely.

GERALDINE: But now, as soon as I've made my cocoa ... kitchen out here, Stella?

STELLA: Yes, but let me ...

GERALDINE: No no, I'll find everything – then I think, Paul, we should go back to bed, so we can be asleep for the alarms to wake us up.

PAUL: Absolutely – and really looking forward to that.

GERALDINE: And the cocoa is where, Stella?

STELLA: In the press to the left of the cooker ... but let me ...

GERALDINE: No no. You don't want a cocoa or ... *(POINTED)* anything to drink, do you, darling?

PAUL: To drink? No no, I'm fine – I only came down be-cause of the bang.

GERALDINE: *(PROMPTING)* You're sure?

PAUL: What? Well, maybe then I'll join you in a cocoa.

GERALDINE: A cocoa! *(RESIGNED)* Right. Fine. Back in a minute.

	(GERALDINE GOES INTO THE KITCHEN)
PAUL:	*(THEN)* Sorry about that – I thought she'd gone to the loo – but she must have left her damn sleeping pills at home – lying awake up there, eyes wide open, watching me like a hawk.
STELLA:	Paul, I don't think you should stay ...
PAUL:	But Chirst, she has some intuition, hasn't she? – I don't mind saying this to you, Stella – one thing about us, we could always talk – but she's quite right, I really could do with a drink tonight
STELLA:	Oh good. Well if you want to ...
PAUL:	What? No no, I *do* want it, but I can't: I take one and then a few and then we lose the Japanese Four-Ball and where am I then? – my contract is on some Director's desk and there's all these little bastards coming up behind me, snapping at my heels – and wouldn't they just love to see me with the shakes, missing six-inch putts and all those Japanese big-wigs looking on – Jesus, I might as well commit hari-kari there and then. This is all just between you and me now ...
STELLA:	Oh of course ...
PAUL:	But I know exactly *why* I want it – I've been work ing it out and it's simply that if I had come here to-night and seen you happy, I'd be grand – I'd leave here in the morning feeling tip-top ...
STELLA:	But I am happy and ...
PAUL:	Oh for God's sake, Stella, I'm not blind – okay, I know we can't have our chat here now ...
STELLA:	Paul!
PAUL:	*(CLOSE)* But honestly now, do you ever consider this – do you ever think it could have been different if ...
STELLA:	*(ANNOYED)* Paul, Geraldine is out there and Dermot is due back and ...
PAUL:	*(PETULANT)* Right. Fine. Sorry. Bad timing. Forget I said anything. Sorry.
STELLA:	*(GUILTILY)* No, I'm sorry ...
PAUL:	What I might do is pour myself out a small whiskey, if you don't mind ...

STELLA:	Oh no, go ahead, please do ...
PAUL:	*(POURING IT)* I'm only going to pour it out – I'm not going to drink it.
STELLA:	No? Because you can if you wish.
PAUL:	No ... If I just pour it out, hold it in my hand, I'll be fine. I've done this before. It's no problem. And I know it'll really help me.
STELLA:	Because I don't mind if you ...
PAUL:	*(HOLDING HIS DRINK)* And what I want you to do, Stella, is just think about this. If we can't have our little chat now – and clearly we can't – why don't we arrange to meet somewhere, somewhere nice and cosy ...
STELLA:	Oh no ...
PAUL:	I know a lovely place in Kildare – it's quiet and discreet where nobody ...
STELLA:	No, absolutely no, Paul ...
PAUL:	Stella, for Christ sake, I'm only asking that we meet ... maybe have a meal ...
STELLA:	No, I couldn't ...
PAUL:	Just say we can meet and talk – what harm is there in that?
STELLA:	The answer is 'no', Paul.
PAUL:	You have no idea what this place in Kildare is like: its own grounds, a small river, over-hanging trees, little rabbits darting around ...
	(LIGHTS ACROSS THE WINDOW. THE SOUND OF A CAR)
STELLA:	*(PANIC)* Oh my god, here's Dermot! Get Geraldine, go back up to your room ...
PAUL:	Just say 'yes'. No one need ever know ...
STELLA:	No, Paul, I've absolutely no intention of going anywhere with you.
PAUL:	No Stella, you don't mean that.
STELLA:	I do mean it ... *(RUNS TO PUT HER DRINK BACK)*
PAUL:	*(FOLLOWS)* No, say you don't mean it.
STELLA:	All right, I don't mean it. Just go! Now, please, before ...
PAUL:	We'll meet – I can make all the arrangements ...
STELLA:	Dermot is coming! Please ...!

PAUL: Just say 'yes'.
STELLA: Yes yes yes, all right!
PAUL: That's great, Stella. What about early next week?
                 What about Monday?
STELLA: Will you please go!
                 (THE HALL DOOR SLAMS)
PAUL: *(OF HIS GLASS)* Here hold that.
                 *(STELLA ANXIOUSLY TAKES THE GLASS. PAUL
                 MOVES AWAY. DERMOT COMES IN. HE IS CON-
                 FIDENT AND PLEASANT. HE PUTS THE SHOT-
                 GUN ASIDE, TAKES OFF HIS COAT, AS)*
STELLA;   *(GUILTILY)* Ah Dermot, is everything all right?
DERMOT: Everything couldn't be better Stella, all sorted out.
                 Ah Paul, still up, are you?
PAUL: Yes. Well no. I mean yes I am now – we did go to bed
                 but Geraldine came down to make cocoas for her-
                 self and myself and I ...
                 *(GERALDLINE COMES FROM THE KITCHEN,
                 STUNNING IN HER LOW-CUT NIGHT-DRESS,
                 NOW CARRYING TWO CUPS OF COCOA. DER-
                 MOT LOOKS AND CANNOT BELIEVE HIS EYES)*
GERALDINE: Ah Dermot, is everything all right?
PAUL: *(INDICATING)* They're the two cocoas.
DERMOT: *(LOOKS. THEN)* Oh right. And yes, Geraldine,
                 everything is great – all sorted out.
GERALDINE: Oh I'm so glad.
STELLA: And you saw Tara, did you?
DERMOT: I did, *and* Tommy – had a great chat with them just
                 before they disappeared into Jury's, swallowed-up
                 by all their friends.
STELLA: Oh thanks be to God.
DERMOT: That's a thing about kids, Paul – you never know
                 them until you see them with their friends.
PAUL: I'm sure that's very true.
DERMOT: *(PROUDLY)* And Stella, is our Tara popular?
STELLA: Is she?
DERMOT: And Tommy. Another lesson for us there – never
                 jump to conclusions about kids. I take total blame, I
                 never gave him a chance to explain – but the truth
                 about Tommy is that he *does* fix punctures but what

	he didn't tell us is that his father partly-owns Nestors Garage, that Tommy is only serving his apprenticeship and one day he'll own the whole place.
GERALDINE:	*(IMPRESSED)* Own Nestor's garage?
DERMOT:	And two other garages on the south-side. And why did he not tell us this? – because we never asked him.
PAUL:	*(LIGHTLY)* Well why would we?
DERMOT:	Exactly what I said to him, Paul. So I apologised to both of them – and also took the liberty of apologising on both your behalfs.
GERALDINE:	Oh thank you, Dermot.
DERMOT:	But they took it well – you know kids – and I gave them both a big hug and said 'Okay, put all this behind you – go on in and have the time of your lives.'
PAUL:	And so say all of us.
DERMOT:	Absolutely. And so now, with that out of the way – we can settle in and turn our attention to Jupiter.
GERALDINE:	*(ANXIOUS)* Except, Dermot, we were thinking of going back to bed.
PAUL:	*(TO GERALDINE)* We don't really have to ...
GERALDINE:	Oh yes we do.
DERMOT:	Well, have a drink first – I'm going to have one – I think a large brandy would slide down very nicely. What about yourself, Geraldine?
GERALDINE:	Well I already have my cocoa ...
DERMOT:	Okay. Is that a whiskey you have, Stella?
STELLA:	What? Oh this? No. Yes. Yes, I poured it out by mistake.
DERMOT:	*(TAKES IT)* You don't want that, do you? *(PUTS IT INTO PAUL'S HAND)* You can have it, Paul.
PAUL:	Actually no, I don't think so ...
DERMOT:	It might be a Scotch – give it a sniff and see if you'd fancy it.
PAUL:	No, really, honestly, no.
STELLA:	You could bring it to bed with you.
DERMOT:	*(TAKEN ABACK)* Sorry, Stella?
STELLA:	No, I was just suggesting that Paul ...
PAUL:	*(FINALLY)* No, really, I've no intention of drinking

154

	that or anything else, here or in bed or anywhere. Thank you.
GERALDINE:	*(ANGRILY)* Fine! Well then we may as well just go up and lie down and get some rest or whatever we want to do. *(GOING)*
PAUL:	Exactly, great idea, hopefully get in some sleep. *(GOING)*
DERMOT:	*(SEES THE BOOKS)* Oh and don't forget your enclycopaedias.
PAUL:	Didn't I bring those up already?
GERALDINE:	Sorry darling, I brought them down again – I thought you'd read yours.
PAUL:	I haven't opened it yet. Goodnight so.
GERALDINE:	Goodnight.
DERMOT:	*(BRIGHTLY)* Goodnight. And listen out for the alarms.
PAUL:	*(OFF)* Don't worry, we will. *(THE SLIDE-DOOR IS CLOSED)*
DERMOT:	*(QUIETLY, ANGRILY)* Pair of gobshites. *(DERMOT GOES TO CHECK HIS COMPUTER, FAXES, ETC. – ALL AS)*
STELLA:	*(UNEASILY)* They just came down because she wanted to make cocoa.
DERMOT:	*(CONTROLLED)* So I heard.
STELLA:	*(THEN)* And that's great, Dermot, about Tara and Tommy – that they're all right and everything.
DERMOT:	Do you still have your contact lenses in?
STELLA:	What? Oh yes, I do.
DERMOT:	And not hurting you now, are they not?
STELLA:	No, they're grand.
DERMOT:	Very convenient.
STELLA:	Pardon?
DERMOT:	Very convenient that they've stopped hurting you as soon as Paul starts wandering around.
STELLA:	What? No, it was you, Dermot, who told me to keep them in and, as I said, it was Geraldine who came down to ...
DERMOT:	I know, Stella, I know! – and it takes two people to make cocoa, does it?
STELLA:	No – Geraldine first came ...

DERMOT:	And now you're on whiskey – I never heard of you having whiskey before.
STELLA:	No, I poured it out my mistake ...
DERMOT:	And then all your little jokes about him taking it to bed.
STELLA:	*(THEN)* Is everything all right, Dermot? *(THE FAX BEGINS TO PRINT)*
DERMOT:	*(ANGRILY)* Well you tell me, Stella – I run out of here because our daughter is gone off in a hearse with a drug-pusher to god-knows-where and when I come back I find you all in here having the time of your lives ...
STELLA:	Dermot, we weren't ...
DERMOT:	... her making cocoa, him showing off his chest, you half-tipsy and no bother with your contact lenses anymore, chatting away to him, dishing out the drinks and your face as red as beetroot for some unknown reason ...
STELLA:	No that's just the heat in here ...
DERMOT:	The heat? Oh, talking about that, was he? *(READS HIS FAXES)*
STELLA:	Dermot, please, shouldn't we be grateful that Tara is safe ...
DERMOT:	God alone knows how safe Tara is.
STELLA:	But you said you saw her ...
DERMOT:	You wanted me to say in front of him that I could not catch up with them? That my car wouldn't go as fast as a hearse?
STELLA:	So did you not ...?
DERMOT:	And wouldn't he love to hear about me going into the Gresham and asking if they'd seen a hearse arriving and my daughter getting out of it.
STELLA:	The Gresham? But the Debs is in Jurys.
DERMOT:	I know that now, Stella.
STELLA:	But 'Jurys' was written on the tickets ...
DERMOT:	*(QUIETLY FURIOUS)* Meaning what, Stella? Meaning I can't read? Are you now saying I was let go because I couldn't read? Jesus, it gets better and better. *(POURS A DRINK FOR HIMSELF)*
STELLA:	So you never went to Jurys?

156

DERMOT:	I did when they'd all gone in ... I saw the hearse parked outside if that's any consolation.
STELLA:	But you didn't actually see Tara and Tommy ...?
DERMOT:	Christ, next you'll be asking me did he really tell me his oul fella owns Nestors Garage.
STELLA:	But you just told us he part-owns ...
DERMOT:	And how could he tell me that if I didn't see him?! – do you think he left a message at the hotel-desk with the information?
STELLA:	So does he not ...?
DERMOT:	*(HARD)* No Stella, he doesn't! He fixes punctures, he's on the dole, he's a drug-pusher, he drives an un-insured hearse, he's a drop-out, a bum! And if you want it all, O'Mahony's dog, that we're supposed to be minding, is dead! – run down by that same gobshite in his bloody hearse, in his desperation to get away with Tara. I had to shoot her on my way back.
STELLA:	Shoot who?
DERMOT:	Well hardly shoot Tara! Shoot Judy, the dog! The mercy of God I saw her just now on my way back, lying by the bridge where he'd hit her and left her lying there to die, anyway she liked.
STELLA:	Oh my God, the O'Mahonys loved that dog.
DERMOT:	Yes and he mowed her down – that's what we're dealing with here. The mercy of God I had my shot-gun to put her out of her misery.
STELLA:	That was the shot we heard.
DERMOT:	Oh did you – well I hope it didn't disturb you too much.
STELLA:	And what about Tara? – when is she coming home ...?
DERMOT:	God knows when she's coming home or how she's coming home or what happens to her before she comes home or if she ever comes home at all. And if that's not enough, I have a dead dog in the car waiting to be buried. And look, there's e-mail giving me star-chart positions, there's thousands on the Internet waiting for the first pictures of Jupiter and the comet, there's Harold ...

STELLA: *(SUDDEN FURY)* Oh for Christ sake, forget about Jupiter and that fool Harold and all the bloody comets and for once in your life, think about me and our daughter!
(SILENCE. STELLA IMMEDIATELY CONTRITE. DERMOT UNFORGIVING)

DERMOT: *(COLDLY)* I see. And these, I presume, are the additional thoughts of the great Paul?

STELLA: No Dermot, I'm sorry, I didn't mean all that – I'm just so worried in case Tara ...
(DERMOT HAS BEGUN TO PUT HIS COAT ON AGAIN)

DERMOT: Well, it's good to know where everyone stands.

STELLA: Where are you going now?

DERMOT: Do you ever listen, Stella, do you? O'Mahony's dog, that Tara doted on, that the junkie ran-down, is in my car with its legs broken and a bullet in its brain. I don't know about you, but I care enough about Tara not to let her see it.

STELLA: But you're not going to bury it now, are you?

DERMOT: No, I'm going to hang it over the hall-door so she can walk into it.

STELLA: But there's not enough time before Jupiter ...

DERMOT: And another thing – as soon as Jupiter is finished, I want those two gobshites out of the house and gone home.

STELLA: Gone home? But we invited them for the night.

DERMOT: For them, the night will be over about half-past-four – a quick cup of tea, a mouthful of sandwiches, and off with them.

STELLA: But they'll want to talk to Tara ...

DERMOT: Think, Stella! If they see her, they'll see him and where'll I be then with my cock-and-bull story about Nestor's Garage and the puncture-fixer. For once, will you just do what you're told and let me handle everything.

STELLA: But couldn't they just go back to bed for a few hours ...?

DERMOT: Christ, you're so bloody concerned about them – with your contact lenses and your 'drink it in bed'

	– but I'm telling you that they're going home, end of story! Now don't touch anything – the telescope, the computer, my charts, nothing. *(GETS A SPADE FROM THE HALL-WAY, AS)*
STELLA:	Dermot ...
DERMOT:	And let's at least allow Jupiter to salvage something from this night.
	(DERMOT GOES. THE HALL-DOOR CLOSES)
STELLA:	*(FURIOUSLY TO HERSELF)* Jupiter! Do you ever think about anything else, do you? And you don't want my contact lenses in, do you not? Right. Right. Fine. Out they come – suits me, I never wanted the bloody things anyway. *(TAKES OUT HER CONTACT LENSES AND FLINGS THEM ACROSS THE ROOM)* And you don't like my glasses, do you not? Well tough – I like them and I'm going to bloody-well wear them, even when I'm sleeping I'll wear them! *(PUTS ON HER GLASSES)* But don't touch your telescope or your bloody computer or say a bad word about that mad-man Harold. And you want me to kick Geraldine out into the night? – well you can forget that! *(TO THE SLIDING DOOR)* And you, Paul, you can forget it too; you and your Japanese Four-Ball and your little hotel in Kildare and the little bastards snapping at your heels. *(ANGRILY POURS A DRINK)* Well who cares? – not me because I have had enough! And I'll say this to your faces, word for word, I'll scream it at all of you. *(STOPS. THEN WEARILY)* Except, of course, I won't, because all I can ever do is apologise. Forty-three years of age and I'm still apologising to everybody. I can see it all now: one day I'll finish up sitting here apologising to the sheep and goats ... *(SLEEPILY, GOES TO THE SETTEE)* ... telling them about Tara gone off to college, Dermot in looking at the stars and doing his Open University Course and me, still here, living out what's left of my life, apologising ... and the sheep and goats will all look at me, with their big dopey eyes, and they'll all say ... *(DROWSILY)* ... 'And who's to blame for that?'

(THROUGHOUT THIS, STELLA HAS TAKEN OFF HER SHOES AND LAY ON THE SETTEE, A TAR-TAN RUG ACROSS HER. THE LIGHTS DIM AS SHE NOW SLEEPS ... AND SOFT, TINKLING PIANO-MUSIC CREEPS IN. OUTSIDE, BEYOND THE CONSERVATORY, A MAJESTIC IMAGE OF JUPITER APPEARS IN THE HEAVENS – WAIT-ING. ESTABLISH AND HOLD. THEN THE SLIDE-DOOR SLOWLY OPENS AND PAUL COMES FURTIVELY DOWN. HE IS AS BEFORE: SHOES, OPEN SHIRT, TROUSERS.

HE GOES QUIETLY TO THE KITCHEN AND LOOKS IN. THEN TO THE CONSERVATORY AND LOOKS OUT. THEN, SATISFIED, COMES TO WHERE STELLA SLEEPS. HE PLACES A HAND ON HER SHOULDER. SHE JUMPS, SMALL SCREAM, FRIGHTENING PAUL AS MUCH AS HERSELF. CUT MUSIC, IMAGE OF JUPITER, AS)

PAUL:	*(QUIETLY)* Shhhhh – it's only me.
STELLA:	Paul! Where did you ...? what time is ...? is the comet ...?
PAUL:	Easy, easy. The alarms haven't gone off yet.
STELLA:	Where's Dermot?
PAUL:	He's outside – I've been watching him: he's digging a hole.
STELLA:	Oh yes, that's right. *(PUTS ON HER SHOES)*
PAUL:	You know about this?
STELLA:	Yes ... he said he'd be doing that, to keep himself occupied. And Geraldine – is she ...?
PAUL:	In bed – she couldn't remember if she turned off the cooker, so I said I'd check.
STELLA:	And why didn't *she* check it?
PAUL:	Because I insisted – and she was already in bed ...
STELLA:	Then you'd better go back up or she'll come down to see ...
PAUL:	She won't because I locked the door.
STELLA:	You what?
PAUL:	It's okay, if she checks I'll say I did it through force of habit.
STELLA:	So you haven't actually been in bed yet?

160

PAUL:	No, I've been watching Dermot digging a hole.
STELLA:	Oh Christ, this is hopeless.
PAUL:	What? No, Stella, relax, there's no problem ...
STELLA:	*(ANNOYED)* Paul, there are huge problems and I really can't stand much more of this: Geraldine is waiting for you ...
PAUL:	No she's not.
STELLA:	*(PANIC)* Of course she is and the alarms will go off and Dermot will be in from digging and I'm sick and tired of being at the beck and call of everyone: you, Dermot, Geraldine, Tara, everyone.
PAUL:	Stella, for God's sake, you'll make yourself ill ...
STELLA:	A lot you care whether ...
PAUL:	Of course I care – that's why I'm down here to say I'm sorry for interfering and that we have to be realistic: what happened between us is over. You are married, I am married, end of story.
STELLA:	*(DEFUSED)* What?
PAUL:	That's it and we may as well face it. All over and done – and no sense in us planning anything together: chats, that little place in Kildare, the peace and quiet, the little walks down by the river, the rabbits, all that – all over and done.
STELLA:	*(THEN)* Oh. Right.
PAUL:	Good. *(GENTLY)* And I like your glasses.
STELLA:	Oh these? I just ..
PAUL:	They're nice. Always thought glasses suited you.
STELLA:	*(GENTLY)* Oh thanks.
PAUL:	*(PLAYFULLY)* Always thought they made you look studious as well as, well, sexy.
STELLA:	Paul, I think you'd better go before Geraldine ...
PAUL:	Right, absolutely right. *(THEN)* It just seems a shame, doesn't it? – in that there is really nothing left between Geraldine and me ... like, I could be down here all night and she wouldn't miss me.
STELLA:	No no, she would.
PAUL:	No – she never does. A sleeping pill every night and she's gone. There's never anything.
STELLA:	*(WEAKLY)* What?
PAUL:	The truth is, Stella – and I can tell you this because

	we could always talk – but it didn't last – Geraldine and me. Not in a real sense. But I seriously think we would have lasted.
STELLA:	*(DRINKS)* No, we wouldn't – remember I used to just annoy you.
PAUL:	*(LIGHTLY)* No, you made me laugh ...
STELLA:	No, remember even at that Dinner Dance you were really annoyed because I wouldn't ... do anything, or anything ... and then you went off with Geraldine ...
PAUL:	That wasn't the reason I went ...
STELLA:	Come on, admit it, Paul, I wasn't your type, I wasn't pretty enough, I was always too fat for you.
PAUL:	What are you saying? – you were lovely and I didn't mind whether ...
STELLA:	*(EMOTIONAL)* No, Paul, you *did* mind because all I could ever do was try to be funny and Geraldine was lovely and slim ...
PAUL:	*(ARM AROUND STELLA)* All right maybe she was but she never had what you had: personality, a good nature and, most important, someone you'd just want to be with all the time.
STELLA:	*(GENTLY)* What?
PAUL:	Absolutely. And I am certain if you hadn't gone off with Dermot, we'd've got back together again.
STELLA:	No ...
PAUL:	*(CLOSER)* We would ... Okay, I admit, it used to annoy me that you were always on your guard, always afraid of the consequences ...
STELLA:	You used to be furious ...
	(SUDDENLY DERMOT WALKS INTO THE ROOM. HE STOPS DEAD, SEEING WHAT IS HAPPENING. HE HASN'T BEEN SEEN BY EITHER PAUL OR STELLA. HE IMMEDIATELY RETREATS OUTSIDE AGAIN. ALL AS)
PAUL:	But that's all in the past now – we've grown up, matured, learned – you'd have nothing to fear now, nothing, everything taken care of.
STELLA:	No no, Paul ...
PAUL:	Okay, let me try something here.

162

STELLA:	What?
PAUL:	Just something.
STELLA:	No no, I've drunk too much.
PAUL:	Just don't move for just a minute.
	(AS PAUL REACHES FOR STELLA'S GLASSES, DERMOT'S FACE SUDDENLY APPEARS AT THE WALL-WINDOW – UNSEEN BY STELLA OR PAUL)
STELLA:	What are you ...?
PAUL:	Don't move.
	(PAUL TAKES HER GLASSES OFF)
PAUL:	Now that's nice ... very nice.
STELLA:	What is?
PAUL:	Like most people who are short-sighted, you have the most beautiful eyes.
STELLA:	But you said you liked my glasses.
PAUL:	I do – but I like this too. *(STROKES STELLA'S HAIR)* This is like a woman letting her hair down, maybe symbolically baring herself a little bit more ...
STELLA:	I'm only baring my face ..
PAUL:	*(A SMALL KISS ON HER CHEEK)* It's a start, isn't it?
STELLA:	*(GENTLY)* Paul, I don't think you should be doing that ...
PAUL:	*(CLOSE TO HER)* No? Then why have you been trying to get me to drink, eh?
STELLA:	What?
PAUL:	Come on, Dermot's just been messing pushing the drink – but you've been really trying ...
STELLA:	No ...
	(AS PAUL TURNS TOWARDS THE WINDOW, DERMOT DUCKS OUT OF SIGHT, AS)
PAUL:	You remember, don't you?
STELLA:	Remember what?
PAUL:	What I was like with a few drinks – sex-mad you used to say.
STELLA:	Excuse me, Paul, I was never trying to get you to drink to ...
PAUL:	*(GENTLY)* Okay Okay. But admit this – drink or no drink, we did have good times ... and then it all went wrong. Why was that, Stella?

163

	(DERMOT'S FACE RE-APPEARS IN THE WALL-WINDOW)
STELLA:	*(GENTLY)* I don't know.
	(PAUL WILL NOW PUT STELLA'S GLASSES INTO HIS SHIRT POCKET. DERMOT WILL SEE THIS, AS)
PAUL:	Nor do I. But there's still time to find what we lost then. It's not too late. We can still make time for ourselves, we can still find a world in which we're not afraid anymore.
STELLA:	How?
PAUL:	Maybe what I was saying earlier. *(CLOSER)* Maybe giving ourselves a chance to see how we really feel, to do it gently and slowly – maybe in that place I spoke about in Kildare – it's really nice and ...
	(DERMOT'S FACE DISAPPEARS FROM THE WALL-WINDOW. HE DELIBERATELY MAKES A NOISE AND THEN COMES IN. PAUL HEARS THIS IN TIME AND IS INTO ANOTHER CHAIR. FROM NOW, WE WILL NOTICE THAT, WITHOUT HER GLASSES, STELLA CAN SEE VERY LITTLE. ALL AS)
DERMOT:	*(PLEASANTLY)* Ah Paul – up again, are you?
PAUL:	Ah, Dermot!
DERMOT:	Or is Geraldine down again, making more cocoa in the kitchen?
PAUL:	What? No no. In fact I just came down because she couldn't remember if she'd turned off the cooker so I said I'd check.
DERMOT:	Oh right. And had she – turned it off?
PAUL:	Oh yes – so I was just talking to Stella until you came back from ... from ... *(STOPS)*
STELLA:	I was saying you were out digging a hole.
DERMOT:	Oh thank you, Stella.
STELLA:	Because Paul had seen you.
PAUL:	I'd seen you from the bedroom window – Stella was saying it relaxes you.
DERMOT:	Yes. Digging holes at night – did you ever hear of that form of relaxation, Paul?
PAUL:	*(AWKWARDLY)* No.

164

DERMOT:	Very popular in the country, Paul, but don't try it in the city or you'll be arrested.
	(STELLA HAS BEEN FEELING FOR HER DRINK)
	Are you still wearing your contact lenses, Stella?
STELLA:	What? Me? No – I took them out to have a sleep before ... Paul came.
DERMOT:	Oh, right. And shouldn't you be wearing your glasses then?
STELLA:	Oh yes, I should ... I will.
DERMOT:	Not lost, are they?
STELLA:	What? No. No, I just left them ... somewhere. Did you see them, Paul?
PAUL:	Me? No. Can't say I did. *(LOOKS VAGUELY AROUND)*
DERMOT:	Well I'm sure they'll turn up. Any word from Harold?
STELLA:	Oh, I didn't look ...
DERMOT:	Not to worry. But you'll need your glasses to see all that, darling.
STELLA:	*(ANXIOUSLY)* Yes. I know.
PAUL:	*(AWKWARDLY)* Okay. So, I may as well go back to bed.
DERMOT:	Hardly worth while now – the alarms will go off any minute.
PAUL:	Oh right – except that, when they do go off, Geraldine may be wondering where I am ...
DERMOT:	But won't she just come down?
PAUL:	What? *(DEFEATED)* Oh yes. Of course she will.
DERMOT:	*(CASUALLY)* And reminiscing about old times were you, just now?
PAUL:	What?
DERMOT:	Old times – the four of us, the Dinner Dance, and all that.
PAUL:	*(AWKWARDLY)* No no, I don't think so. Were we, Stella?
STELLA:	No ...
DERMOT:	Not reminiscing about the old times when it was me and Geraldine and *(POINTED)* ... you and Stella?
PAUL:	No. No, I just think that we were just remembering how we were all good friends together, you and

	me, all of us, always.
STELLA:	Yes.
DERMOT:	Like at work? – you and me old pals at the office, down all the years, you at one desk and me at the next, few laughs every now and then ... me helping you out and you helping me out. All those times?
PAUL:	Yes, exactly. Look, I think I will go up to Geraldine in case she ... *(MOVES)*
DERMOT:	Then maybe you'd go up *after* you look for my wife's glasses, Paul.
PAUL:	*(STOPS)* What?
DERMOT:	Stella said she has lost her glasses ...
STELLA:	No, I just misplaced them ...
DERMOT:	No no, you'll need your glasses, Stella – and Paul won't mind helping us, will you, Paul?
PAUL:	What? Okay, if you want. *(COMES BACK TO IDLY LOOK AROUND THE ROOM)*
STELLA:	Dermot, please, it really doesn't matter.
DERMOT:	*(SWEETLY TO PAUL)* Yes, let's all look everywhere and let's keep on looking until we find them – and when we find them and depending *where* we find them, I may very well decide to smash your smug little face into the back of your head.
PAUL:	*(STOPS. TO DERMOT)* What did you just say?
DERMOT:	*(HARD)* Which, I now realise, is what someone should have done to you a long time ago ...
PAUL:	*(ANGRILY)* For God's sake, what the hell is this – what's got into you now?
STELLA:	Please Dermot, I can explain ...
DERMOT:	*(CONTROLLED ANGER)* Well Paul, as you've asked, I'll tell you exactly what's got into me – first of all it's you, two years ago sitting in the office, looking at me clearing out my desk and you knowing I was years senior to you ...
PAUL:	*(ANGRILY)* For God's sake, we're not back to this, are we?
DERMOT:	Oh, it bothers you, does it?
PAUL:	No it doesn't bother me because you opted for the Redundancy Package ...
DERMOT:	*(FURIOUSLY)* I opted for nothing – my job was axed

166

	for you to jump in and grab all my duties.
PAUL:	We were de-layering the company, we were down-sizing the workforce ...
DERMOT:	'We'! You were once my Union Representative!
PAUL:	*(AGGRESSIVELY)* Okay – how much did you walk out with?
DERMOT:	I walked out with nothing ...
PAUL:	A pension and fifty thousand pounds!
DERMOT:	*(LOUDER)* I walked out with nothing except time on my hands and phoney sympathy from all you bastards ...
PAUL:	And fifty K.
	(PAUL ANGRILY POURS HIMSELF A WHISKEY, AS)
DERMOT:	... and when I went back to see you, you were all too busy to talk to me, too busy to even look up from your new VDU's, to even say hello – all suddenly too busy to leave your telephones and your fax machines and your bloody computers ...
PAUL:	For Christ sake, you'd left, you were gone – what were you running back for?
DERMOT:	I never left, I was pushed out and I was the senior man ...
PAUL:	Face up to it, you were the weakest member of the team ...
DERMOT:	And you were the drunkest member of the team ...
PAUL:	I was never drunk ...
DERMOT:	Look at you! Look at you!
PAUL:	I can take it or leave it. *(REALISES – PUTS THE GLASS DOWN)*
DERMOT:	But I gave my whole life to that job, and they let you grab everything ...
PAUL:	I grabbed nothing ...
DERMOT:	And now you think you can walk in here and grab my wife as well ...
PAUL:	Your wife? Don't talk rubbish!
DERMOT:	I saw you, I saw you!
PAUL:	I don't want your bloody wife ...
STELLA:	Let me explain.
PAUL:	... I happen to have a wife of my own.

DERMOT:	*(TO PAUL)* I was shaggin looking at you ...
PAUL:	*(AGGRESSIVELY)* But if I *did* have her I'd treat her a lot better than you ...
DERMOT:	Oh would you?
STELLA:	Stop it!
PAUL:	Yes I would and I wouldn't be dragging her up into this empty life ...
DERMOT:	This isn't an empty life – she loves this life ...
PAUL:	Just look at her.
DERMOT:	What's wrong with her?!
PAUL:	Are you blind or something?
STELLA:	*(ANGRILY)* Don't talk as if I'm not here.
DERMOT:	Well at least I gave her children.
STELLA:	Stop it!
PAUL:	One child.
DERMOT:	Which is more than you gave your wife ...
PAUL:	And what a child – out tonight with a dressed-up drug-pusher.
DERMOT:	He's not a drug-pusher ...
PAUL:	Owns a garage, does he?
DERMOT:	His father half-owns ...
STELLA:	*(AS THEY CONTINUE)* Stop it, stop it, stop it ...
PAUL:	Christ, do you think we're fools? He fixes punctures, he's another failure, just like you, – that's your problem, Dermot, you attract failures to you.
DERMOT:	That's it – I'll take no more of this ... *(DERMOT RUNS AT PAUL. THE FIGHT IS ANGRY AND VICIOUS. FURNITURE KNOCKED OVER. IMMEDIATELY, THE ALARMS RING AND CONTINUE, AS)*
STELLA:	Will you stop it! *(PICKS UP DERMOT'S ASTRONOMY TROPHY. NOW LOUD AND ANGRY – AND FULL OF FEARFUL HYSTERIA)* Dermot, stop it, stop it or I'll smash this to pieces. *(DERMOT AND PAUL SEE HER AND STOP. THE ALARM BELLS STOP, AS)*
DERMOT:	*(CONTROLLED)* Now Stella, you listen to me – that is a very delicate and valuable trophy and it's not mine so ... so just put it down.
STELLA:	*(BARELY CONTROLLED)* No, I'm serious, Dermot

	– I've had enough of all of this …
GERALDINE:	*(OFF)* Paul, the door is locked.
PAUL:	*(CALLS)* Okay Geraldine, I'm coming … *(MOVES)*
STELLA:	*(HARD)* Leave her, Paul, leave her!
PAUL:	*(STOPS)* I beg your pardon?
STELLA:	Or who are you going to say locked her in there?
PAUL:	What? I'll say I did, by mistake.
STELLA:	And I'll soon tell her what was a mistake and what wasn't – and Geraldine won't like that – she has great intuition, hasn't she, Paul?
DERMOT:	*(FURY)* Jesus, you locked your wife in the bedroom so you could … *(RUNS AT PAUL)*
STELLA:	*(LOUDLY)* Dermot, shut up or I'll smash this to smithereens …
DERMOT:	*(TURNS TO STELLA)* No, you will not, Stella – you will give me that trophy this instant because the alarms for Jupiter have gone off and I …
STELLA:	*(FURIOUS)* And would it surprise you, Dermot, to know that I don't give a damn about Jupiter because the same Jupiter and that head-case Harold get more attention in this house than I do …
DERMOT:	*(OF THE TROPHY)* Will you stop waving it around!
STELLA:	… and it's not going to continue because I want changes around here and I want them from tonight!
DERMOT.	And I want that trophy and I want it now! *(MOVES)*
STELLA:	*(RETREATING)* I'll throw it, Dermot, I swear I'll throw it …
DERMOT:	No you will not throw it …
STELLA:	I will, Dermot …
	(STELLA THROWS IT. [IDEALLY, WE SHOULD SEE IT THROWN AND BROKEN. OTHERWISE, IT IS THROWN BEHIND THE SETTEE] DERMOT FREEZES. THEN GOES TO IT. STELLA STANDS BACK VICTORIOUSLY … WILL THEN MOVE TOWARDS THE TELESCOPES. A FAX BEGINS TO PRINT OUT. DERMOT PICKS UP THE BROKEN TROPHY – PIECES HANGING LOOSE)
DERMOT:	*(STUNNED)* Jesus Christ, Stella – that's the Solar System. I have to give that back …
PAUL:	*(STUNNED)* You really shouldn't have done that,

	Stella.
STELLA:	I warned you ...
DERMOT:	Stella, I can never forgive you for this. *(PLACES IT BACK IN ITS POSITION)*
STELLA:	*(ANGRILY)* And next is the telescope if you are still not listening.
	(STELLA HAS NOW TAKEN HOLD OF THE BIG TELESCOPE)
DERMOT:	*(PANIC. PLEADING)* Jesus Christ, Stella, don't touch the telescope!
GERALDINE:	*(OFF)* Paul, are you watching Jupiter?
PAUL:	*(SHOUTS)* Shut-up Geraldine. *(THEN)* Sorry, darling – no, we're not.
STELLA:	I won't touch anything, Dermot, if you just listen.
DERMOT:	All right, I am, I am listening. *(TO THE CONTINUING FAX MACHINE)* Christ, Harold, will you just wait for me! *(TO STELLA)* Look, I'm listening, Stella, but that camera has to be activated and if you even touch that telescope we would have 200 photos of either the ceiling or, worse, the bloody Wicklow Hills.
STELLA:	So are you listening?
DERMOT:	Yes yes, I'm listening – just don't ... all right, go on, I'm listening, I'm listening.
STELLA:	First and foremost, I want my glasses – I can't see a thing here. Paul?
PAUL:	Me? But I don't ...
STELLA:	*Now*, Paul – unless you want Geraldine to ...
PAUL:	Oh yes. *(TAKES THEM FROM HIS POCKET)* I found them on the chair when she ... *(GIVES THEM TO STELLA)*
DERMOT:	Jesus, do you think I'm a fool – you bloody-well took them off her ... *(TOWARDS PAUL)* ... and for that alone, I'm going to break every bone in your body as soon as I tell your wife ...
STELLA:	*(GRABS THE TELESCOPE AGAIN)* Dermot!
DERMOT:	*(PANIC. PLEADING)* Yes, Stella, yes, I'm listening, I'm listening – but don't don't ... just tell me what you want, for Christ sake.
STELLA:	First, I want no more arguing from anyone tonight

...

DERMOT:	All right all right, and what else?
STELLA:	And I want you to understand that Paul found my glasses on a chair, where I left them.
DERMOT:	*(RESIGNED)* Oh I see. Yes, I think I know where I stand now.
STELLA:	So you have nothing to tell Geraldine.
DERMOT:	Great.
STELLA:	And I want both of them to stay here tonight and, after they have seen the comet, to have a good night's rest.
DERMOT:	Terrific.
STELLA:	And Paul, you *are* staying the night, aren't you? – after we all watch Jupiter – you and Geraldine?
PAUL:	To be perfectly honest ...
STELLA:	*(HARD)* You are! And Dermot, later on, I'd like to talk about us moving back to Terenure.
DERMOT:	*(FURIOUS)* Fine, Stella – and anything else? Like, where the hell is our marriage, once you've sobered up?
STELLA:	But now, would you go up to Geraldine, unlock the door and tell her that *you* locked it by mistake.
DERMOT:	Me?
STELLA:	Yes, and not Paul – and let her come down and watch Jupiter.
DERMOT:	Oh yes, that's it, look after him, cover up for him ...
STELLA:	Just do it, Dermot.
DERMOT:	No problem, Stella, whatever you say. But you will live to regret this night – because this is the end of us – this, I will never forgive. Never!
	(DERMOT GOES UPSTAIRS. PAUL RELAXES, AMUSED. POURS A DRINK)
PAUL:	Well well well – isn't this more like the Stella we all once knew.
STELLA:	And loved?
PAUL:	Absolutely. It is actually good to see you like this – brings it back to me – that spirit. And thanks for covering-up about the glasses and that locked door. That was nice. *(THEN)* I always knew that Dermot couldn't be easy to live with – so don't you forget

171

	what I was saying about us, our little get-together, that place in Kildare – one phone-call and that can all be arranged, it's as easy as that. *(THEN)* But right now, Stella, I really think we should leave well-enough alone, quietly say our farewells, and Geraldine and I will slip away before ...
STELLA:	Oh no, Paul, I would prefer if you stayed here tonight.
PAUL:	*(FLATTERED)* Oh? Would you really?
STELLA:	Yes – I think Geraldine would like both of you to stay.
PAUL:	Well maybe she would, but I personally ...
STELLA:	Paul, what would it take to keep you here tonight?
PAUL:	*(PLAYFULLY)* Well, what are you suggesting?
STELLA:	Well, supposing your new car was punctured – then you'd have to stay, wouldn't you?
PAUL:	Well yes, but it's not. Those cars are ...
STELLA:	Then you watch carefully, Paul – watch out for that spirit you admire so much, watch it in action... *(STELLA HAS PICKED UP THE SHOT-GUN AND CLOSED IT. SHE WILL NOW GO QUICKLY OUT THROUGH THE CONSERVATORY)*
PAUL:	Stella, what the hell are you ...?
STELLA:	You watch very carefully now ...
PAUL:	*(AFTER HER)* Now you wait a minute, Stella, you hold it right there – that gun could be loaded, Stella – this is not funny ... you've had too much to drink ... *(SHE AIMS AND FIRES)*
STELLA:	*(VICTORIOUSLY)* Yes! Bulls-eye!
PAUL:	Jesus Christ, what the hell have you done? *(RUNS IN, HEADING FOR THE ENTRANCE DOOR)* You bloody mad bitch – I always wondered about you – you and your dopey daughter and your thick husband ... *(DERMOT AND GERALDINE RUN DOWN THE STAIRS. GERALDINE NOW WEARS A SENSIBLE, HEAVY SWEATER OVER HER NIGHT-DRESS)*
DERMOT:	Stella, what happened?
PAUL:	*(AS HE PASSES)* Your mad wife has tried to blow

DERMOT:	my car away ...
DERMOT:	What?
PAUL:	*(TO DERMOT)* If there is the slightest damage to that car, you are in trouble – very very big trouble. *(PAUL RUNS OUT)*
DERMOT:	*(FURIOUSLY TO STELLA)* Terrific! *(RUNS AFTER PAUL)*
GERALDINE:	Jesus Stella, have you lost your mind ...
STELLA:	He was going to go home – he said he wanted to go home and you ...
GERALDINE:	*(ANGRILY)* Then why didn't you just let me ask him – instead of your husband locking me in my room. That is so stupid, Stella – his car! Of all things! – what are you thinking of? What's going to happen to me now? Stupid! *(RUNS OUT)* Paul? Darling?
DERMOT:	*(COMES ANGRILY IN)* Happy now, are you? Finished destroying everyone, have you?
STELLA:	*(HAND TO HER FOREHEAD)* Dermot, I just wanted to ...
	(IMMEDIATELY A NEW SIREN IS HEARD – FOR THE CRASH ON JUPITER. FROM NOW, THE LARGE IMAGE OF JUPITER APPEARS BEYOND THE CONSERVATORY WINDOWS ... AND THE SKIES WILL FLASH WITH RED ... ALL AS)
DERMOT:	My God, the crash has started! Activate roof! *(THROWS THE SWITCH – THE CONSERVATORY ROOF OPENS AGAIN)* Activate camera! *(SWITCHES ON THE AUTOMATIC CAMERA ON THE TELESCOPE. RUNS TO HIS COMPUTER. PUNCHES KEYS TO BRING IMAGE OF JUPITER ONTO SCREEN)* I suppose you didn't check to see if Jupiter was showing ...?
STELLA:	Dermot ...
DERMOT:	Of course you didn't – why should that concern you – you have your old flames to think of, your lovers quarrels ... but we're finished, Stella, you know that, don't you? Finished!
STELLA:	*(SLUMPING TO THE FLOOR)* Dermot, please ...
DERMOT:	*(AT HIS TELESCOPE)* Oh for God's sake, we're out

	of focus – I'm photographing nothing.
PAUL:	*(OFF)* Oh my God, look what she's done!
DERMOT:	Stella, did you move this, did you? – I can see nothing.
STELLA:	Dermot, I don't feel well ...
DERMOT:	I had this spot-on – Jesus Christ, what'll they think of me ...
PAUL:	*(OFF)* Where is he? Let me at him!
	(IF POSSIBLE IN PRODUCTION, THE SCREEN IMAGE IS NOW BLURRED, AS)
DERMOT:	*(ADJUSTING THE TELESCOPE)* Hey, wait a minute ... come on ... come on ...
STELLA:	Dermot, please help me – I'm not well.
	(THE ALARMS FADE BUT NOW WE HEAR THE THUNDERING COMET. THROUGH THE CONSERVATORY WINDOW, THE IMAGE OF JUPITER REMAINS, MAJESTIC AND SPECTACULAR. [IF POSSIBLE, ON THE COMPUTER SCREEN, THE 'SNOWY' IMAGE CLEARS AND JUPITER IS CLEARLY SEEN IN THE HEAVENS – THE IMAGE THAT DERMOT NOW SEES THROUGH HIS TELESCOPE, THAT WE SEE THROUGH THE CONSERVATORY] EVERYWHERE SEEMS TO BE EXPLODING IN RED FLASHES. ALL AS)
STELLA:	Please ...
DERMOT:	*(AT THE TELESCOPE)* Yes! Yes! Beautiful! There she is – Jupiter! Yes, these will be great pictures, Stella – Yes! Beautiful! Oh you beautiful lady!
GERALDINE:	*(OFF)* Now Paul, let's talk to him ...
PAUL:	*(OFF)* I'll beat the shit out of him ...
GERALDINE:	*(COMING IN)* No darling – let me get you a drink first ...
PAUL:	*(COMING IN. FURIOUS TO DERMOT)* You! Gobshite! Have you seen my car? Have you seen what your stupid wife has done?
GERALDINE:	*(POURING A DRINK)* Here, darling, drink this.
PAUL:	*(SHOUTS)* You! The man in the shaggin moon – I'm talking to you. *(TAKES THE DRINK)*
	(GERALDINE WILL NOW URGENTLY TAKE OFF HER HEAVY, UNSEXY SWEATER AND PREPARE

	FOR BED, AS)
DERMOT:	*(AT HIS TELESCOPE)* Paul, Harold's comet is pounding into Jupiter at this very moment ...
PAUL:	You come out and see my car or I'll be pounding into you ...
DERMOT:	Look, twenty photographs so far ...
PAUL:	Are you deaf or something ...
GERALDINE:	Drink, Paul – go on, drink-up darling ... *(SUDDENLY STOPS. SEES STELLA, SLUMPED AND IMMOBILE ON THE FLOOR)* Stella! Stella, are you all right? Dermot! Quick!
PAUL:	*(SEES STELLA)* Jesus Christ what the hell happened to her?
GERALDINE:	She just collapsed ... She's ashen ... *(CALLS)* ... Dermot, she looks really bad ... is there a doctor anywhere ...?
PAUL:	Oh Jesus ... she's not ...? Is she breathing? Is she? *(TO DERMOT)* She doesn't look as if she's breathing!
GERALDINE:	Oh my God. *(DERMOT, SUDDENLY AWARE, HAS LEFT HIS TELESCOPE, COME TO STELLA, NOW KNEELS BY HER, HOLDING HER HAND)*
DERMOT:	*(CONCERNED)* Stella? Are you all right? Oh Stella. Stella ... please. Please say you're all right. Stella, please. Please ... Stella ... oh Stella, please?

(GERALDINE AND PAUL STAND, WATCHING – GERALDINE WITH HER ARMS AROUND PAUL. HE RESPONDING. DERMOT DISTRAUGHT. STELLA IMMOBILE.

AS THE LIGHTS GO DOWN, THE THUNDERING NOISE FADES ... AS WE FADE TO BLACKOUT)

END OF SCENE ONE. ACT TWO

ACT TWO. SCENE TWO

(DARKNESS AND PEACE. EARLY-MORNING BIRD-SONG. NOW LIGHTS UP – THE LIGHT OF DAWN THROUGH THE WINDOWS. THE ROOM IS IN ORDER, THE ASTRONOMY TROPHY, LOOKING PERFECT, IS IN POSITION, AS BEFORE. NO SIGN OF CONFLICT.

STELLA IS ASLEEP ON THE SETTEE AS ON PAGE 160. AS THEN, SHE HAS THE TARTAN RUG AROUND HER, HER SHOES BESIDE THE SETTEE. SHE IS NOW WAKING – HEARING AND IDENTIFYING EVERYTHING. SHE PUTS ON HER GLASSES AND LOOKS AROUND, AT THE ROOM, AT THE TROPHY. NOW REALISES)

STELLA: Oh thank God, it was all a dream. I'm still here on the sofa. *(REALISING)* Oh thanks be to God. I fell asleep when Dermot went out to bury the dog ... dreamed that Paul came back down to me! *(SMALL LAUGH)* ... oh, I might have known that was a dream – me standing up to them like that. *(LOOKS AROUND)* Dermot must have come back and found me asleep and ... and left me to wait for Tara ... *(CHECKS HER WATCH)* Wonder if she's back yet? Quarter past seven. Still in Bewley's I suppose ... *(NOW MORE UNSURE)* And Jupiter? Don't tell me I slept through them all watching Jupiter! And Geraldine and Paul ...?

    (SHE HEARS GERALDINE SINGING QUIETLY AND HAPPILY SOMEWHERE. ASSUMES THAT THE SOUND COMES FROM UPSTAIRS – BUT THEN GERALDINE COMES FROM THE KITCH-EN. SHE IS DRESSED IN SMART DAY CLOTHES. SHE HAS A MUG OF COFFEE. SHE IS IN GREAT HUMOUR)

GERALDINE: *(MERRILY)* Ah, awake at last – you must give me details of what you were drinking – I could use that for one of my sleepless nights. Oh, I helped myself to some coffee ...

STELLA: *(CONFUSED)* Oh yes, of course.

GERALDINE: *(SITS)* Get some sustenance for the cold morning

	air. And don't you get cold there – Dermot said he'd fix the heating later – something minor, he said. But God, Stella, what a night, eh? And aren't you a wild child when you get going?
STELLA:	*(UNSURE)* Am I?
GERALDINE:	And now, I know what you are dying to ask me, so ask me.
STELLA:	Yes – did I really ... did I?
GERALDINE:	*(STOPS)* Really what?
STELLA:	Did I break anything ... the trophy looks all right.
GERALDINE:	You don't remember Dermot trying to fix it?
STELLA:	Oh my God. And where is Dermot? Did he get to photograph Jupiter? Where's Paul? *(GETS UP)*
GERALDINE:	Wooooooo. I wouldn't stand too quickly – you've been out cold for ages. Do you remember us coming back in?
STELLA:	*(SITS)* Back in where?
GERALDINE:	In here, after you blew-out Paul's tyres?
STELLA:	*(NOW REALISES)* Oh my God.
GERALDINE:	We thought you were dying – we just stood there frozen and Dermot running around like a lunatic, wondering whether to ring a doctor or not ...
STELLA:	I don't remember ...
GERALDINE:	*(LAUGHING)* ... you waking up for a minute to tell him to photograph Jupiter and he saying 'To hell with Jupiter – how is my little Stella, my Stella By Starlight' – and Paul immediately said, 'Hey, *that* was the name of that dreary song at the Dinner Dance – it's Stella by Starlight, not Gaslight' – it was all priceless.
STELLA:	And where's Dermot now?
GERALDINE:	They're out changing the wheel. Paul said the back one was a slow puncture and should get us as far as Dublin. Then they said they'd hoover-up the broken glass off the seats.
STELLA:	Oh my God. And what about Jupiter – did Dermot ...?
GERALDINE:	Stella! Every question but the right question!
STELLA:	What? Oh yes – you and Paul – did he ...?
GERALDINE:	*(DELIGHTED)* Yes! *(THEN)* Okay, he had to have a

	whiskey – well, actually, he took the whole bottle up with him – he said he needed it to get over his anger at what you did to his car ...
STELLA:	I'm so sorry ...
GERALDINE:	No no – once he started drinking he was as randy as a little mongrel – more tricks than you'd see in Duffy's Circus – and who cares if, eventually, he didn't know who the hell I was, I still made sure when he finished that he remembered what he'd done, and to whom – and so, instant pregnancy.
STELLA:	Oh I'm so glad for you.
GERALDINE:	And I can tell you this has saved my life, my marriage, my sanity, it has made this whole trip worthwhile – and it will do Paul the world of good: he's always wanted kids – this will make all the difference. *(QUIETER)* Pity he's back on the booze – but that's another day's work.

(DERMOT AND PAUL COME IN. PAUL, NOW DRESSED IN SMART CASUAL CLOTHES, IS CLEARLY THE WORST FOR WEAR: HAIR TOSSED, WEARING DARK GLASSES – BUT HAPPY. DERMOT COOL AND POLITE)

PAUL:	*(TAKING DIRECTIONS)* So, left at the bridge and straight on to the fork and then left down the valley and up again at the right ...?
DERMOT:	... and the next sharp left with the road a bit hidden on your right ...
PAUL:	Okay okay, I have that – I'm pretty good on directions ...
GERALDINE:	Ah darling – she's awake.
PAUL:	Oh good. Feeling better, Stella?
STELLA:	Hello Paul, hello Dermot ...
DERMOT:	Stella – all right, are you?
STELLA:	Yes, Dermot, I'm grand.
DERMOT:	The migraine didn't come back or ...?
STELLA:	No no – and Paul, I'm very sorry about your car ...
PAUL:	*(OFF-HAND)* Oh that's all okay, Stella – glad you've recovered, sobered-up, whatever – and I'm glad to say that I think Dermot and I have sorted everything out ...

DERMOT: Yes – Paul has agreed to claim all car damages from his insurance ...

PAUL: Yes, no problems there – *(THE DEAL)* and Dermot, don't you want to ...?

DERMOT: Oh yes – apologies again, Geraldine, for locking you in your room.

GERALDINE: Oh I'd forgotten completely about that.

PAUL: *(THE DEAL)* Good. Excellent. And really sorry, Dermot, we missed seeing Jupiter ...

DERMOT: *(WEAKLY)* Yes, pity.

PAUL: *(AMUSED)* But Geraldine, we must put it in our diaries to come up and see the eclipses of Mercury and Venus. When are they again, Dermot?

DERMOT: *(COLDLY)* Two thousand and twelve.

PAUL: Won't feel the time passing. So, we'll be on our way ...

STELLA: Really? You won't wait until Tara ...?

DERMOT: *(DETERMINED)* No, they won't – Paul says he's very exhausted after last night.

PAUL: *(HUGS GERALDINE)* Exhausted is not the word.

GERALDINE: *(LOVINGLY)* Oh yes it is, lover-boy.

PAUL: *(LOVINGLY)* Little devil. *(THEN)* Oh, and my photo. *(TAKES THE DINNER DANCE PHOTO. CONSIDERS. THEN)* Maybe best to leave the past in the past, eh? *(TEARS IT)* But, Dermot, hope your Jupiter pictures come out well – and give our love to Tara and also to young ... *(AMUSED)* ... Needles. Wish him luck with all his ... puncture-fixing.

DERMOT: *(NOT AMUSED)* I will.

PAUL: Bye Stella. *(DELIBERATELY SHAKES HANDS, RATHER THAN KISSES HER)* Take care.

STELLA: Yes. Bye, Paul.

DERMOT: Your bag is out here, Paul.

PAUL: *(GOING)* Great. And drop into the office sometime – we'd love to see you – always good to see an old face.

DERMOT: Right, I must. *(GOING)*

PAUL: Do. And a lovely house. Lovely area. No chance of the Dart ever coming out this way, is there? *(PAUL AND DERMOT GO)*

GERALDINE: *(KISSES STELLA)* Stella, I'll give you a buzz in the next week or so.

STELLA: Oh do. And I'm really glad about everything.

GERALDINE: All thanks to you – *(QUIETLY)* and listen, I've been thinking, about the baby, if it's a boy I'd like to call him Paul, but if it's a girl, I'd really like to call her ...

STELLA: *(HUMBLY)* No no, really, there's no need to call her Stella.

GERALDINE: Stella? Oh God no, of course not. I think, for Paul's sake, I might call her 'Pauline'. That's what I'm hoping for and it's such a sweet name – and he'd like that. See you.

STELLA: *(COOLER)* Yes, Geraldine.

(GERALDINE GOES. THE CAR STARTS UP AND GOES, BLOWING ITS HORN. STELLA WAITS ANXIOUSLY FOR DERMOT TO RETURN)

STELLA: *(TO HERSELF)* And now. And now. And now.

(DERMOT COMES IN)

DERMOT: *(ANGRILY)* Couldn't wait to get out of here, the bastard – and all his spoofing, all his sarcastic talk. And you, Stella, down here with him when my back was turned.

STELLA: I wasn't doing anything.

DERMOT: Oh he assured me of that a million times out there – when he wasn't giving me all his other tricks of the trade. Bloody whore-master.

STELLA: Dermot, nothing happened.

DERMOT: And what about the trophy?

STELLA: The trophy looks all right.

DERMOT: Oh it is, it's great ... *(PICKS TWO BALLS LYING BESIDE IT)* ... provided you don't expect to see Earth or Venus in our Galaxy. It's bloody destroyed, Stella. *(TRIES TO PICK IT UP. IT FALLS TO PIECES)* And not a word from Harold since I sent the pictures. And you collapsing in the middle of it all. *(ANGRILY)* Bloody house, bloody shack, bloody miserable backwoods of the country, always something wrong somewhere.

STELLA: *(THEN)* Dermot, if we moved back to Terenure ...

DERMOT: *(ANGRILY)* Ah for God's sake, not that.

STELLA:	But Dermot, you love Dublin – I know you do – you love being able to buy your newspaper ... and the book-shops ... the astronomy society ... and I could probably get my old job back in the bank there and ...
DERMOT:	And I'm not listening because three guesses who I've just seen driving up the valley.
STELLA:	It's not Tara, is it? Is it? *(GOES TO THE CONSERVATORY)*
DERMOT:	One car-load of trouble drives out, another drives in.
STELLA:	*(LOOKING)* Oh thank God, it's the hearse.
DERMOT:	Such a place – now a hearse arriving is good news.
STELLA:	*(LOOKING OUT)* They're both sitting in the front.
DERMOT:	And if that Needles-fellow decides to come in here ...
STELLA:	I'm sure he will, Dermot.
DERMOT:	Good, because as soon as we've established that he hasn't pumped Tara with drugs, I intend to, firstly, confront him with driving over O'Mahony's dog and leaving it to die on the road-side ...
STELLA:	Well maybe not if they're tired.
DERMOT:	*(ANGRILY)* Tired or not tired, I then want to know why he's called Needles, why he drinks water, why he thinks Ecstasy Tablets are a joke – and I want Tara to see him for what he is: a dosser, a junkie and a dog-killer and I want her to be rid of him. And I want this house back to how it was before this blasted Debs.
	(VOICES ARE NOW HEARD, QUIETLY, OUTSIDE)
TARA:	*(OFF)* Quiet or you'll wake them ...
TOMMY:	*(OFF)* Ah Jaysas, I nearly stepped into that cow-pat.
TARA:	*(OFF)* There's no cows up here.
TOMMY:	*(OFF)* What is it then – the Abominable Snowman? Snowman-shit, is it?
TARA:	*(OFF)* Quiet!
TOMMY:	*(OFF)* Oh, I forgot to put the hand-brake on.
TARA:	*(OFF)* You're a messer. Don't bang the door coming in ...
	(TARA HAS ALREADY ENTERED – TIRED AND

	HAPPY, SLIGHTLY DISHEVELLED, WEARING
	TOMMY'S BOW-TIE – SHE NOW STOPS IN
	FRIGHT ON SEEING STELLA AND DERMOT)

TARA: Mum, what are you doing up ... and Dad!

STELLA: Hello Tara, is everything all right?

TARA: Course it is – except that I'm absolutely out of it.

DERMOT: *(ANXIOUSLY)* You're what, Tara?

TARA: I'm tired, daddy. Mum, I asked Tommy in for a minute.

STELLA: Of course – make some coffee, inside in the kitchen. *(QUIETER)* And was it good?

TARA: It was brilliant, mum, just brilliant. An absolute rave – the best ever.

(TOMMY COMES IN. HE TOO LOOKS A LITTLE DISHEVELLED – NO JACKET, SHIRT OPEN AND WEARING TARA'S WRAP AROUND HIS WAIST)

TOMMY: Oh hello there.

TARA: They're both here to meet us.

DERMOT: Yes, to meet you and to ask a few questions.

STELLA: Dermot!

TOMMY: *(MERRILY)* Well, all the answers will be the same – we had a brilliant time. But we just saw your man driving away from here ...

TARA: *(AMUSED)* Stop, Tommy!

TOMMY: And I was saying that the comet you were looking at must have missed Jupiter, and hit his bleeding car.

(GREAT LAUGHTER FROM TARA AND TOMMY)

DERMOT: *(ANGRILY)* Very humorous – but, if you don't mind, I'd prefer answers to the questions I *want* answered. Like, Needles, where exactly did this colourful name come from and why are you called it.

TARA: Oh daddy, not now.

DERMOT: Yes, now, Tara!

TARA: *(ANGRILY)* But that all goes back years ...

TOMMY: No, it's all right ...

TARA: Oh for God's sake!

TOMMY: It was just a name they gave me ...

TARA: Daddy, you don't want all this after my Debs ...

DERMOT: I bloody-well do want it.

182

TOMMY: It's no sweat. It's something that started when I was eleven when I was always fainting and they said I had too much sugar in my blood so the doctor said I had to inject myself and when me little brothers seen all these needles, they gave me the name and it stuck – but I don't mind and I'm grand now anyway.

TARA: Of course you are – you're terrific. *(HARD)* Satisfied, dad?

DERMOT: *(BACKING QUICKLY DOWN)* What? Oh right. Grand. Matter of fact, that's what I suspected – just wanted your confirmation.

TOMMY: No sweat.

STELLA: All right, Tara, take Tommy in for a coffee.

DERMOT: *(HARD AGAIN)* But before you do that, you don't mind if we have a word about O'Mahony's dog ...

STELLA: Oh Dermot for Heaven's sake!

DERMOT: No Stella ...

TARA: Yes, where is she, Daddy – did you lock her up for the night?

TOMMY: Because Tara was looking for her just now.

DERMOT: *(TO TOMMY)* Oh was she?

TARA: Yes, because when we were going, she chased us all the way to the bridge and we had to stop and I got out to hoosh her back, but she wouldn't move and we had to leave her standing in the middle of the road, looking after us ...

TOMMY: ... And I said that the next car that comes around that corner would smack into her ...

TARA: ... Except there's never any cars up there at night and, unless they were driving like lunatics, she'd get out of their way in time.

TOMMY: *(TO DERMOT)* Why, did she not run back to the house after?

(DERMOT LOOKS AT STELLA. NOW REALISES)

STELLA: *(THEN)* No, she didn't actually ... run ... back – but maybe she is back at O'Mahony's. Is she, Dermot?

DERMOT: *(SHATTERED)* What?

TOMMY: Well if there's nobody there, she'll be back here rapid – soon as she gets hungry again.

TARA: Course she will. Why what did you want to ask us

	about her, dad?
DERMOT:	What? Oh nothing.
TARA:	But you said you wanted to ask Tommy ...
STELLA:	That's all right, Tara – I think we're all a bit tired for that now. In you go now, the two of you, and not for too long.
TARA:	Okay, mum.
	(TOMMY AND TARA GO LOVINGLY INTO THE KITCHEN)
DERMOT:	It was me ... Oh Jesus Christ, Stella, it was me that killed her, I killed O'Mahony's dog.
STELLA:	No, Dermot, maybe someone else ...
DERMOT:	It had to be me – she was alive when they saw her at the bridge, I was doing seventy going after them ... I must have hit her then ...
STELLA:	It wasn't your fault ...
DERMOT:	*(DISTRAUGHT)* I ran her down, Stella: the dog the O'Mahony's idolise, that they asked us to look-after so they'd have peace of mind in Florida – first, I ran her down, then I came back and I shot her and then I buried her in my front garden! How can I explain that to them now?
STELLA:	We don't have to say anything about ...
DERMOT:	*(IN DESPAIR)* And I was blaming him – calling him a junkie when the poor devil's a diabetic ... and the one thing Harold asked me to do, I could not do properly ... and the trophy they presented to me, I'll be giving back to them in bits – I'm useless ... bloody useless ... the office was right, why wouldn't they get rid of me? – look at me, look at this bloody house ... useless, bloody useless.
STELLA:	No Dermot, it was probably me ...
DERMOT:	No no, it's me, and it's bloody everything: losing my job, getting you to give up your job, forcing you and Tara to come up here, getting you to stick lenses in your eyes, giving you migraines ...
STELLA:	They don't give me ...
DERMOT:	And I don't blame you for Paul – not one bit – I knew all along it was him – from the time you asked him to that bloody Dinner Dance, I always knew.

STELLA:	Dermot, I've already explained ...
DERMOT:	*(APOLOGETIC)* I know, I know, Stella, I'm sorry, it's me, it's me, I know that. *(THEN)* And he'll be after you again – he's an insatiable whore-master – I got it all out there while we were changing his wheel – all his accomplishments: the places to get it, the young-wans who'll give it to you, the kind of after-shave to use ... and the things Geraldine knows nothing about: his mysterious credit cards .. and the secret vasectomy he had ... everything.
	(DERMOT SITS, HEAD IN HANDS. STELLA STUNNED)
STELLA:	*(THEN)* Dermot, what did you just say about Paul?
DERMOT:	Oh yes – Mr Success.
STELLA:	Did you just say he had a vasectomy?
DERMOT:	And I know what you're thinking, Stella – what a fool I was slagging him about having no children and he making sure he couldn't possibly have any. Bet he had a laugh at that too.
STELLA:	And Geraldine doesn't know?
DERMOT:	No more than she knows about a hundred other things – and don't you go telling her.
	(STELLA, REALISING, SLOWLY SHAKES HER HEAD)
DERMOT:	And Stella, I know Wicklow has been a failure – you were right all along and we may as well slink back to Terenure with our tails between our legs.
STELLA:	No, not as failures, Dermot ... but as people who are willing to give something a go ...
DERMOT:	And when Terenure doesn't work, we'll be off again and again and again ... all I've ever done for you, Stella, is to drag you down, all these years – and that's what I can never make up to you.
STELLA:	No Dermot, we'll have friends in Terenure, real friends – and for the first time in two years, we won't be running away.
DERMOT:	I can see Paul's face already ...
STELLA:	Oh forget Paul – they're both a thing of the past. And anyway, wait until I tell you what's ahead for them – you think we have problems! The reason I

asked you about Paul's vasectomy was because Geraldine told me, in strict confidence ...

(TARA COMES FROM THE KITCHEN. TOMMY IS BEHIND HER. BOTH HAVE COFFEES)

TARA: Hey Dad, Tommy was wondering ...

STELLA: A moment, Tara.

          (STELLA WHISPERS TO DERMOT, AS)

TARA: *(MOCK PETULANCE)* Oh excuse me – are you sure we're not in the way here? Like, it was just one simple question that Tommy had for daddy.

TOMMY: It's no sweat if you're busy ...

DERMOT: *(TO STELLA)* What?! And that's why she wanted to get to bed ...?

STELLA: *(QUICKLY TO TARA)* Wait in the conservatory, Tara ... *(CONTINUES TO WHISPER TO DERMOT)*

TARA: *(GOING. TO TOMMY)* God, this is when I really hate them – when they're like this, I might as well be invisible.

STELLA: *(QUIETLY TO DERMOT)* That's why she wanted to get him to drink.

DERMOT: *(QUIETLY TO STELLA)* Yes, but he could just admit that he had it done.

STELLA: *(QUIETLY)* To her?! She'd kill him – she's wanted a baby for years! And if he says nothing, he'll have to live with that baby, knowing that it's not his and she has been ...

DERMOT: *(REALISING)* Oh my God.

TARA: *(AT THE FAX MACHINE)* Hey, dad look, this is from Harold – they got the pictures.

DERMOT: A moment, Tara.

          (TARA, PUZZLED AT DERMOT'S LACK OF IN-TEREST, NOW LOOKS AROUND THE CONSER-VATORY, AS)

STELLA: *(TO DERMOT)* And even if he pretends that it's his, he'll always know that you know that it's not, because he told you about his little you-know-what. *(A SNIPPING GESTURE TO ILLUSTRATE)*

DERMOT: *(REALISING)* Oh Jesus Christ. The poor bastard.

STELLA: And then we're worrying about what they think of us?

TARA:	*(IN THE CONSERVATORY)* Mum, Dad! – they're on their way back.
STELLA:	What? Who are?
TARA:	Your friends – they're driving up the valley.
STELLA:	*(GOES TO SEE)* You're joking – tell me you're joking.
TOMMY:	No, the wrecked car is limping back – look, now with a flat tyre.
DERMOT:	*(PANIC)* Oh good God, I don't believe it, I don't believe they're back again, I don't believe it, I just don't believe it ...
STELLA:	*(GOES TO HIM QUICKLY. CALMING)* It's all right, Dermot, it's all right – we can just let them in, we'll talk to them, we'll put on some coffee, and you can eat your Marietta biscuits if you want to, and we will behave normally.
TOMMY:	And I can fix that puncture for them, get them going again.
STELLA:	Exactly – and Dermot, we don't need to worry about these people anymore.
DERMOT:	*(REALISES)* Yes. You're right. *(TO TARA)* She's absolutely right.
STELLA:	And Tara, you might like to take Tommy back into the kitchen and put on that coffee for me ...?
TARA:	A pleasure, Mum.
DERMOT:	Tommy, before you go, did you say you had a question for me?
TOMMY:	Ah it's okay, it was nothing.
DERMOT:	No no, what was it?
TOMMY:	No, it was stupid.
TARA:	Tommy was just wondering, did Jupiter survive the comet crashing into it last night.
DERMOT:	Jupiter? Oh yes. She'll still be out there just as she was, with maybe a few extra craters ... *(TO STELLA)* ... a few cuts and bruises so to speak. *(TO TOMMY)* ... It's always the comets that come off worst in these crashes.
STELLA:	Okay Tommy? Now inside, Tara. And strong coffee, please.
DERMOT:	And thanks for asking, Tommy – that was a very

	good, intelligent, astronomical question.
TOMMY:	I was just curious – like I'm very interested in that kind of thing.
DERMOT:	*(STOPS)* Are you really?
TOMMY:	Oh yeah. *(PROUDLY)* Like, I would never ever miss looking up my horoscope every morning.
	(DERMOT LOOKS AWAY IN DESPAIR)
TOMMY:	I mean, looking at me now, would you know, off-hand, that I was a Virgo?
DERMOT:	*(DEFLATED)* No Tommy, I wouldn't.
TARA:	Come on, Tommy. See you later, Dad. And Mum, you're still wearing your glasses, if you want to change.
	(TOMMY AND TARA GO INTO THE KITCHEN)
STELLA:	*(TO DERMOT. GENTLY)* Do I need to change?
DERMOT:	*(WARMLY)* I don't see why you should.
	(THE DOOR-BELL RINGS)
STELLA:	Oh Dermot, that's more like it. *(KISSES HIM)* And I don't want you to change either.
DERMOT:	*(THEN)* Stella, are you really so unhappy up here?
STELLA:	Well, I'm not ... *(STOPS. DECIDES)* Yes I am, Dermot. And so are you.
DERMOT:	Me?
STELLA:	Yes, Dermot – you miss Dublin. I know you do.
	(THE DOOR-BELL RINGS AGAIN)
DERMOT:	Better let them in.
STELLA:	Yes. *(STOPS)* Or maybe let them ring again?
DERMOT:	*(DECIDES)* Yes. Good idea. What's the hurry?
	(NOW, AMUSED AT PAUL'S MISTAKE) Stella by Gaslight.
STELLA:	*(WARMLY)* Starlight – and not a dream.

(STELLA AND DERMOT EMBRACE AND, AS THE SONG 'STELLA BY STARLIGHT' IS HEARD AND THE ROOM IS FLOODED IN THE REVOLVING LIGHTS OF A DANCE HALL, THEY BEGIN TO DANCE, SLOWLY AND LOVINGLY, OBLIVIOUS TO THE OUTSIDE WORLD ... AS WE FADE TO DARKNESS)

THE END

NOTES

NOTES